EVOLVE

STUDENT'S BOOK

with Digital Pack

Lindsay Clandfield, Ben Goldstein, Ceri Jones, and Philip Kerr

2A

CAMBRIDGE
UNIVERSITY PRESS

Shaftesbury Road, Cambridge CB2 8EA, United Kingdom

One Liberty Plaza, 20th Floor, New York, NY 10006, USA

477 Williamstown Road, Port Melbourne, VIC 3207, Australia

314–321, 3rd Floor, Plot 3, Splendor Forum, Jasola District Centre, New Delhi – 110025, India

103 Penang Road, #05-06/07, Visioncrest Commercial, Singapore 238467

Cambridge University Press & Assessment is a department of the University of Cambridge.

We share the University's mission to contribute to society through the pursuit of education, learning and research at the highest international levels of excellence.

www.cambridge.org
Information on this title: www.cambridge.org/9781009231800

© Cambridge University Press & Assessment 2019, 2022

This publication is in copyright. Subject to statutory exception and to the provisions of relevant collective licensing agreements, no reproduction of any part may take place without the written permission of Cambridge University Press & Assessment.

First published with Digital Pack 2022

20 19 18 17 16 15

Printed in Dubai by Oriental Press

A catalogue record for this publication is available from the British Library

ISBN 978-1-009-23170-1 Student's Book with eBook
ISBN 978-1-009-23179-4 Student's Book with Digital Pack
ISBN 978-1-009-23180-0 Student's Book with Digital Pack A
ISBN 978-1-009-23181-7 Student's Book with Digital Pack B
ISBN 978-1-108-40898-1 Workbook with Audio
ISBN 978-1-108-40863-9 Workbook with Audio A
ISBN 978-1-108-41192-9 Workbook with Audio B
ISBN 978-1-108-40516-4 Teacher's Edition with Test Generator
ISBN 978-1-108-41065-6 Presentation Plus
ISBN 978-1-108-41202-5 Class Audio CDs
ISBN 978-1-108-40788-5 Video Resource Book with DVD
ISBN 978-1-009-23152-7 Full Contact with Digital Pack

Additional resources for this publication at www.cambridge.org/evolve

Cambridge University Press & Assessment has no responsibility for the persistence or accuracy of URLs for external or third-party internet websites referred to in this publication, and does not guarantee that any content on such websites is, or will remain, accurate or appropriate. Information regarding prices, travel timetables, and other factual information given in this work is correct at the time of first printing but Cambridge University Press & Assessment does not guarantee the accuracy of such information thereafter.

ACKNOWLEDGMENTS

The *Evolve* publishers would like to thank the following individuals and institutions who have contributed their time and insights into the development of the course:

José A. Alvarado Sotelo, **Summit English**, Mexico; Maria Araceli Hernández Tovar, **Instituto Tecnológico Superior de San Luis Potosí**, Capital, Mexico; Rosario Aste Rentería, **Instituto De Emprendedores USIL**, Peru; Kayla M. Briggs, **Hoseo University**, South Korea; Lenise Butler, **Laureate**, Mexico; Lilian Dantas; Aslı Derin Anaç, **İstanbul Bilgi University**, Turkey; Devon Derksen, **Myongji University**, South Korea; Roberta Freitas, **IBEU**, Rio de Janeiro, Brazil; Monica Frenzel, **Universidad Andrés Bello**, Chile; Gloria González Meza, **Instituto Politecnico Nacional, ESCA (University)**, Mexico; Elsa de loa Angeles Hernández Chérrez, **Centro de Idiomas, Universidad Técnica de Ambato**, Ecuador; José Manuel Cuin Jacuinde, **Coordinación de Lenguas Extranjeras del Instituto Tecnológico de Morelia**, Mexico; Thomas Christian Keller, **Universidad de las Américas**, Chile; Daniel Lowe, **Lowe English Services**, Panama; Antonio Machuca Montalvo, **Organización The Institute TITUELS**, Veracruz, Mexico; Daniel Martin, **CELLEP**, Brazil; Ivanova Monteros, **Universidad Tecnológica Equinoccial**, Ecuador; Verónica Nolivos Arellano, Language Coordinator, Quito, Ecuador; Daniel Nowatnick, **USA**; Claudia Piccoli Díaz, **Harmon Hall**, Mexico; Diego Ribeiro Santos, **Universidade Anhembri Morumbi**, São Paulo, Brazil; Maria del Socorro, **Universidad Autonoma del Estado de Mexico, Centro de enseñanza de lenguas (Toluca)**, Mexico; Heidi Vande Voort Nam, **Chongshin University**, South Korea; Isabela Villas Boas, **Casa Thomas Jefferson**, Brasilia, Brazil; Jason Williams, **Notre Dame Seishin University**, Japan; Matthew Wilson, **Miyagi University**, Japan.

To our student contributors, who have given us their ideas and their time, and who appear throughout this book:

Alessandra Avelar, Brazil; Noemi Irene Contreras Yañez, Mexico; Celeste María Erazo Flores, Honduras; Caio Henrique Gogenhan, Brazil; Lorena Martos Ahijado, Spain; Allison Raquel, Peru; Seung Geyoung Yang, South Korea.

And special thanks to Katy Simpson, teacher and writer at *myenglishvoice.com*; and Raquel Ribeiro dos Santos, EFL teacher, EdTech researcher, blogger, and lecturer.

Authors' Acknowledgments:

The authors would like to thank Daniel Isern for all his support in the early stages of the project. This book is dedicated to Groc.

The authors and publishers acknowledge the following sources of copyright material and are grateful for the permissions granted. While every effort has been made, it has not always been possible to identify the sources of all the material used, or to trace all copyright holders. If any omissions are brought to our notice, we will be happy to include the appropriate acknowledgements on reprinting and in the next update to the digital edition, as applicable.

Photos:

Key: B = Below, BG = Background, BL = Below Left, BR = Below Right, C = Centre, CL = Centre Left, CR = Centre Right, L = Left, R = Right, T = Top, TC = Top Centre, TL = Top Left, TR = Top Right.

All images are sourced from Getty Images.

p. xvi (photo 1): Klaus Vedfelt/DigitalVision; p. xvi (photo 2): Cultura RM Exclusive/dotdotred; p. 1: Artur Debat/Moment; p. 2 (Cecilia): Juanmonino/iStock/Getty Images Plus; p. 2: PeopleImages/DigitalVision; p. 2 (Marta): Imanol Lpez/EyeEm; p. 2 (siblings): Michael Prince/Corbis; p. 2 (crowd): John Lund/Blend Images; p. 2 (Marcos): Anthony Charles/Cultura; p. 6 (BL): shapecharge/E+; p. 6 (BR): PeopleImages/E+; p. 7: pixelfit/E+; p. 9, p. 18 (photo a), p. 29 (B), p. 62 (photo c): Bloomberg; p. 10, 20, 30, 42, 52, 62: Tom Merton/Caiaimage; p. 10 (twins): James Woodson/Photodisc; p. 10 (costumes): John Lund/Sam Diephuis/Blend Images; p .10 (graduates): kali9/E+; p. 10 (cooking): Scott T. Smith/Corbis Documentary; p. 11: Geber86/E+; p. 12: T3 Magazine/Future; p. 13: LucaZola/Photographer's Choice; p. 14 (calendar): Iserg/iStock/Getty Images Plus; p. 14 (document): lumpynoodles/DigitalVision Vectors; p. 14 (headphones): deepblue4you/iStock/Getty Images Plus; p. 14 (keyboard): einegraphic/iStock/Getty Images Plus; p. 14 (mouse): jjltd/DigitalVision Vectors; p. 14 (notepad notes): ctermit/iStock/Getty Images Plus; p. 14 (electrical outlet): kostsov/iStock/Getty Images Plus; p. 14 (screen): tovovan/iStock/Getty Images Plus; p. 14 (spine): Irina Kit/iStock/Getty Images Plus; p. 14 (wifi): Amin Yusifov/iStock/Getty Images Plus; p. 14 (park): Maremagnum/

Photolibrary; p. 14 (coffee shop): monkeybusinessimages/iStock/Getty Images Plus; p. 14 (suburban train): VCG/Visual China Group; p. 16, p. 57: Jose Luis Pelaez Inc/Blend Images/Getty Images Plus; p. 17: Westend61; p. 18 (photo b): Ron Dahlquist/Perspectives; p. 18 (photo c): Endre Majoros/EyeEm; p. 18 (photo d): Sharon Mccutcheon/EyeEm; p. 18 (photo e): Oli Scarff/Getty Images News; p. 19 (photo a): RedlineVector/iStock/Getty Images Plus; p. 19 (photo b): RaStudio/iStock/Getty Images Plus; p. 19 (photo c): LCOSMO/iStock/Getty Images Plus; p. 19 (person standing): gece33/E+; p. 20 (teenager): XiXinXing/iStock/Getty Images Plus; p. 20 (female 20s): Dimitri Otis/Taxi; p. 20 (aged female),(male 20s), p.30 (tennis): Hero Images; p. 21: Paul Gilham/Getty Images Sport; p. 22 (team): sampics/Corbis Sport; p. 22 (fans): Africalmages/iStock/Getty Images Plus; p. 22 (score): Wavebreakmedia/iStock/Getty Images Plus; p. 22 (tennis court): David Madison/Photographer's Choice; p. 22 (soccer field): Arctic-Images/DigitalVision; p. 22 (swimming pool): ewg3D/E+; p. 22 (female athelete): Syldavia/iStock/Getty Images Plus; p. 22 (race): Michael H/Taxi Japan; p. 22 (gym): Matthew Leete/DigitalVision; p. 22 (ball net): AFP; p. 22 (3d ball): evrenselbaris/DigitalVision Vectors; p. 22 (3d tennis): medobear/DigitalVision Vectors; p. 24 (photo a): Buda Mendes/Getty Images Sport; p. 24 (photo b): Julian Finney/Getty Images Sport; p. 24 (photo c): Adam Pretty/Getty Images Sport; p. 26 (TR): Kevork Djansezian/Getty Images News; p. 26 (TL): Portland Press Herald; p. 28 (bike riding), p. 30 (basketball): Thomas Barwick/Taxi; p. 28 (bike station): agcuesta/iStock Editorial/Getty Images Plus; p. 29 (black male): JGI/Jamie Grill/Blend Images; p. 29 (old male): Marc Romanelli/Blend Images; p. 29 (black female): Plume Creative/DigitalVision; p. 29 (white female): Dougal Waters/DigitalVision; p. 29 (white couple): Giorgio Fochesato/Photographer's Choice; p. 29 (T): konradlew/E+; p. 30 (running track): Yellow Dog Productions/Iconica; p. 30 (swimming pool): Peter Cade/The Image Bank; p. 30 (soccer): FatCamera/E+; p. 30 (park exercise): AlexSava/E+; p. 30 (mobile screen): Jonathan Daniel/Getty Images Sport; p. 32: Steve Debenport/E+; p. 33: PorasChaudhary/Stone; p. 35: Paul Bradbury/Caiaimage; p. 42 (cat): MASAO OTA/amana images; p. 42 (jewellery): Lisa Bennett/EyeEm; p. 42 (jar): kiboka/iStock/Getty Images Plus; p. 42 (candle): Nicklas Karlsson/EyeEm; p. 43, p. 62 (photo a): Hindustan Times; p. 46 (watch): Davies and Starr/The Image Bank; p. 46 (graduates): EMMANUEL DUNAND/AFP; p. 46 (new employee): MILATAS; p. 46 (couple): photosindia; p. 46 (couple baby): Chris Ryan/OJO Images; p. 46 (question mark): Kritchanut/iStock/Getty Images Plus; p. 46 (map): young84/iStock/Getty Images Plus; p. 46 (stethoscope): MicrovOne/iStock/Getty Images Plus; p. 46 (trophy): Magnilion/DigitalVision Vectors; p. 51: ilbusca/E+; p. 52: Keystone/Hulton Archive; p. 54: Neville Elder/Corbis Historical; p. 56 (photo a): Gerard Fritz/Photographer's Choice; p. 56 (photo b): moodboard/Cultura; p. 56 (photo c): Antenna; p. 58 (electric store): jmalov/E+; p. 58 (pharmacy): JackF/iStock/Getty Images Plus; p. 58 (nail clipper): terex/iStock/Getty Images Plus; p. 58 (adaptor): costinc79/iStock/Getty Images Plus; p. 60 (photo b): drnadig/iStock/Getty Images Plus; p. 60 (photo c): Gregor Schuster/Photographer's Choice; p. 62 (photo b): Scott Olson/Getty Images News; p. 62 (photo d): ROLF VENNENBERND/DPA; p. 64: Steve Stringer Photography/Moment; p. 141 (bottle): thumb/iStock/Getty Images Plus; p. 141 (cream): Anthony Lee/Caiaimage; p. 141 (umbrella): kaisphoto/E+; p. 141 (candy bar): Chee Siong Teh/EyeEm; p. 141 (tissue): Mimadeo/iStock/Getty Images Plus; p. 158 (photo a): Coprid/iStock/Getty Images Plus; p. 158 (photo b): homeworks255/iStock/Getty Images Plus; p. 158 (photo c): LotusWorks/iStock/Getty Images Plus; p. 158 (photo d): bergamont/iStock/Getty Images Plus; p. 158 (photo e): mbtaichi/iStock/Getty Images Plus; p. 160 (photo a): ballyscanlon/Stockbyte; p. 160 (photo b): PC Plus Magazine/Future; p. 160 (photo c): elfinima/E+; p. 160 (photo d): AlexLMX/iStock/Getty Images Plus; p. 160 (photo e): Viktorus/iStock/Getty Images Plus.

The following images are sourced from other sources:

p. 18 (The 7 Habits of Highly Effective People): Courtesy of Franklin Covey Co.

Clipart Courtesy of Noun Project Inc.

Front cover photography by Alija/E+/Getty Images.

Illustrations by: 290 Sean (KJA Artists) pp. 4, 5; Denis Cristo (Sylvie Poggio Artists Agency) p. 12; Ana Djordjevic (Astound US) p. 20; Lyn Dylan (Sylvie Poggio Artists Agency) p. 2; Joanna Kerr (New Division) p. 15; Dusan Lakicevic (Beehive illustration) pp. 15, 25; Liav Zabari (Lemonade illustration) p. 23.

Audio production by CityVox, New York

EVOLVE

SPEAKING MATTERS

EVOLVE is a six-level American English course for adults and young adults, taking students from beginner to advanced levels (CEFR A1 to C1).

Drawing on insights from language teaching experts and real students, EVOLVE is a general English course that gets students speaking with confidence.

This student-centered course covers all skills and focuses on the most effective and efficient ways to make progress in English.

Confidence in teaching.
Joy in learning.

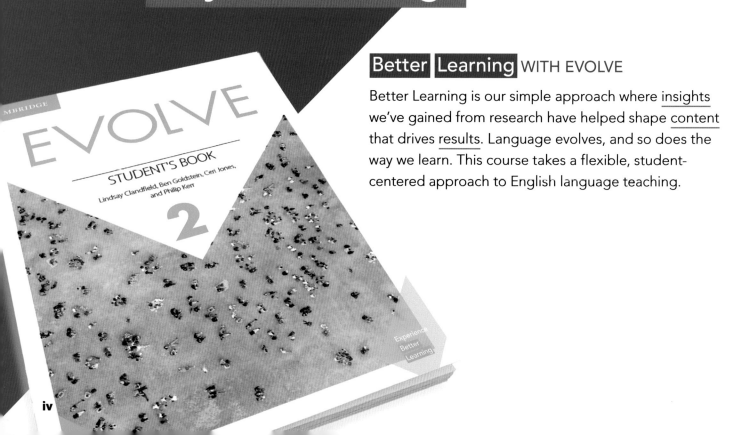

Better Learning WITH EVOLVE

Better Learning is our simple approach where insights we've gained from research have helped shape content that drives results. Language evolves, and so does the way we learn. This course takes a flexible, student-centered approach to English language teaching.

EVOLVE
STUDENT'S BOOK
Lindsay Clandfield, Ben Goldstein, Ceri Jones, and Philip Kerr
2

Meet our student contributors

Videos and ideas from real students feature throughout the Student's Book.

Our student contributors describe themselves in three words.

ALESSANDRA AVELAR
Creative, positive, funny
Faculdade ICESP, Águas Claras, Brazil

NOEMI IRENE CONTRERAS YAÑEZ
Funny, intelligent, optimistic
Universidad del Valle de México, Mexico

CELESTE MARÍA ERAZO FLORES
Happy, special, friendly
Unitec (Universidad Tecnologica Centroamericana), Honduras

CAIO HENRIQUE GOGENHAN
Funny, lovely, smart
Universidade Anhembi Morumbi, Brazil

ALLISON RAQUEL
Friendly, cheerful, intelligent
Universidad Privada del Norte, Peru

SEUNG GEYOUNG YANG
Happy, creative
Myongji University, South Korea

LORENA MARTOS AHIJADO
Cheerful, positive, kind
Universidad Europea de Madrid, Spain

Student-generated content

EVOLVE is the first course of its kind to feature real student-generated content. We spoke to over 2,000 students from all over the world about the topics they would like to discuss in English and in what situations they would like to be able to speak more confidently.

The ideas are included throughout the Student's Book and the students appear in short videos responding to discussion questions.

INSIGHT
Research shows that achievable speaking role models can be a powerful motivator.

CONTENT
Bite-sized videos feature students talking about topics in the Student's Book.

RESULT
Students are motivated to speak and share their ideas.

v

"It's important to provide learners with interesting or stimulating topics."

Teacher, Mexico (Global Teacher Survey, 2017)

Find it

FIND IT

INSIGHT

Research with hundreds of teachers and students across the globe revealed a desire to expand the classroom and bring the real world in.

CONTENT

Find it are smartphone activities that allow students to bring live content into the class and personalize the learning experience with research and group activities.

RESULT

Students engage in the lesson because it is meaningful to them.

Designed for success

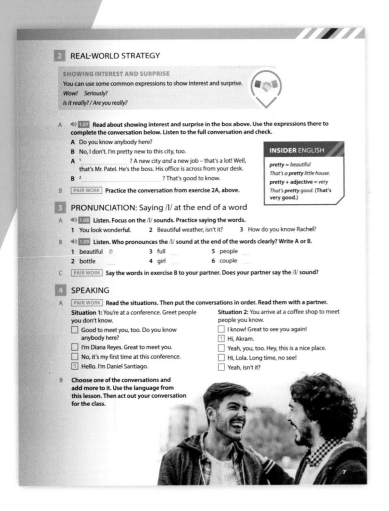

REAL-WORLD STRATEGY

2 REAL-WORLD STRATEGY

SHOWING INTEREST AND SURPRISE
You can use some common expressions to show interest and surprise.
Wow! Seriously?
Is it really? / Are you really?

A 🔊 1.07 **Read about showing interest and surprise in the box above. Use the expressions there to complete the conversation below. Listen to the full conversation and check.**
  A Do you know anybody here?
  B No, I don't. I'm pretty new to this city, too.
  A ¹ _____? A new city *and* a new job – that's a lot! Well, that's Mr. Patel. He's the boss. His office is across from your desk.
  B ² _____? That's good to know.

B PAIR WORK **Practice the conversation from exercise 2A, above.**

> **INSIDER** ENGLISH
> *pretty = beautiful*
> *That's a **pretty** little house.*
> *pretty + adjective = very*
> *That's **pretty** good. (That's very good.)*

3 PRONUNCIATION: Saying /l/ at the end of a word

A 🔊 1.08 **Listen. Focus on the /l/ sounds. Practice saying the words.**
  1 You look wonderful.   2 Beautiful weather, isn't it?   3 How do you know Rachel?

B 🔊 1.09 **Listen. Who pronounces the /l/ sound at the end of the words clearly? Write A or B.**
  1 beautiful B   3 full ____   5 people ____
  2 bottle ____   4 girl ____   6 couple ____

C PAIR WORK **Say the words in exercise B to your partner. Does your partner say the /l/ sound?**

4 SPEAKING

A PAIR WORK **Read the situations. Then put the conversations in order. Read them with a partner.**
Situation 1: You're at a conference. Greet people you don't know.
  ☐ Good to meet you, too. Do you know anybody here?
  ☐ I'm Diana Reyes. Great to meet you.
  ☐ No, it's my first time at this conference.
  1 Hello. I'm Daniel Santiago.

Situation 2: You arrive at a coffee shop to meet people you know.
  ☐ I know! Great to see you again!
  1 Hi, Akram.
  ☐ Yeah, you, too. Hey, this is a nice place.
  ☐ Hi, Lola. Long time, no see!
  ☐ Yeah, isn't it?

B **Choose one of the conversations and add more to it. Use the language from this lesson. Then act out your conversation for the class.**

7

Pronunciation

INSIGHT
Research shows that only certain aspects of pronunciation actually affect comprehensibility and inhibit communication.

CONTENT
EVOLVE focuses on the aspects of pronunciation that most affect communication.

RESULT
Students understand more when listening and can be clearly understood when they speak.

Insider English

INSIGHT
Even in a short exchange, idiomatic language can inhibit understanding.

CONTENT
Insider English focuses on the informal language and colloquial expressions frequently found in everyday situations.

RESULT
Students are confident in the real world.

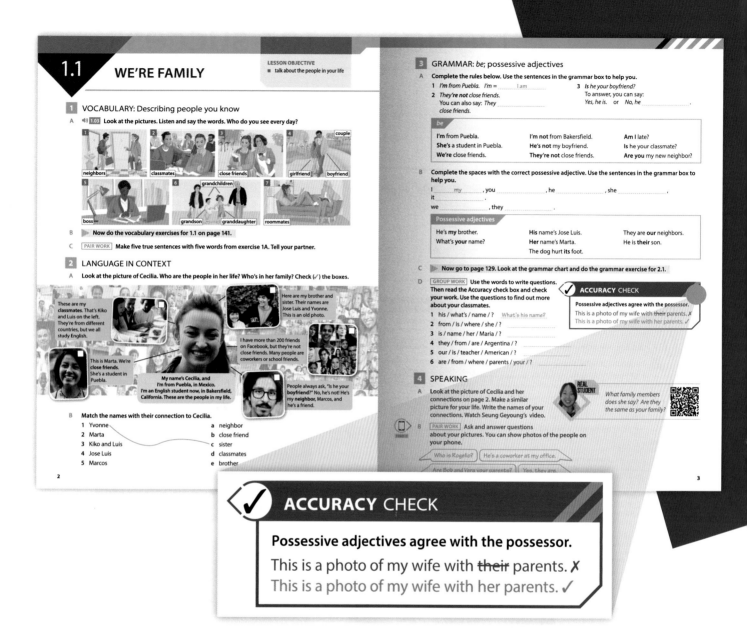

Accuracy check

"The presentation is very clear and there are plenty of opportunities for student practice and production."

Jason Williams, Teacher, Notre Dame Seishin University, Japan

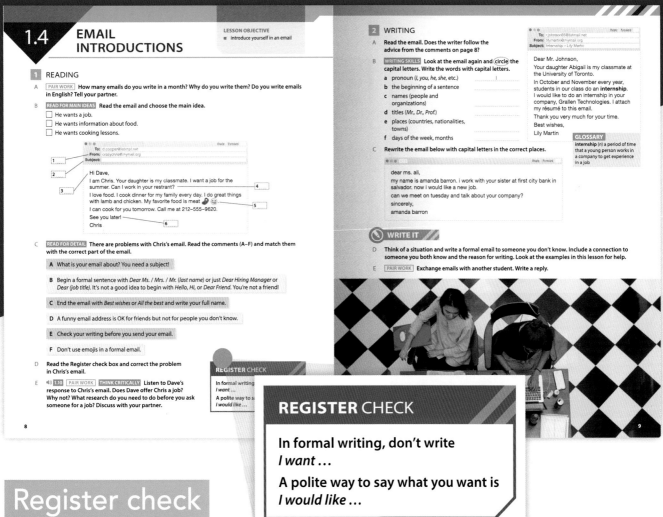

1.4 EMAIL INTRODUCTIONS

LESSON OBJECTIVE
■ introduce yourself in an email

1 READING

A **PAIR WORK** How many emails do you write in a month? Why do you write them? Do you write emails in English? Tell your partner.

B **READ FOR MAIN IDEAS** Read the email and choose the main idea.
☐ He wants a job.
☐ He wants information about food.
☐ He wants cooking lessons.

To: d.cooper@lstmail.net
From: crazychris@mymail.org
Subject:

Hi Dave,
I am Chris. Your daughter is my classmate. I want a job for the summer. Can I work in your restrant?
I love food. I cook dinner for my family every day. I do great things with lamb and chicken. My favorite food is meat 🍖
I can cook for you tomorrow. Call me at 212–555–9620.
See you later!
Chris

C **READ FOR DETAIL** There are problems with Chris's email. Read the comments (A–F) and match them with the correct part of the email.

A What is your email about? You need a subject!

B Begin a formal sentence with *Dear Ms. / Mrs. / Mr. (last name)* or just *Dear Hiring Manager* or *Dear (job title)*. It's not a good idea to begin with *Hello, Hi,* or *Dear Friend*. You're not a friend!

C End the email with *Best wishes* or *All the best* and write your full name.

D A funny email address is OK for friends but not for people you don't know.

E Check your writing before you send your email.

F Don't use emojis in a formal email.

D Read the Register check box and correct the problem in Chris's email.

E 🔊 1.10 **PAIR WORK** **THINK CRITICALLY** Listen to Dave's response to Chris's email. Does Dave offer Chris a job? Why not? What research do you need to do before you ask someone for a job? Discuss with your partner.

2 WRITING

A Read the email. Does the writer follow the advice from the comments on page 8?

B **WRITING SKILLS** Look at the email again and circle the capital letters. Write the words with capital letters.
a pronoun (*I, you, he, she*, etc.)
b the beginning of a sentence
c names (people and organizations)
d titles (*Mr., Dr., Prof.*)
e places (countries, nationalities, towns)
f days of the week, months

To: rjohnson4569@lstmail.net
From: lilymartin@mymail.org
Subject: Internship – Lily Martin

Dear Mr. Johnson,
Your daughter Abigail is my classmate at the University of Toronto.
In October and November every year, students in our class do an **internship**. I would like to do an internship in your company, Grallen Technologies. I attach my résumé to this email.
Thank you very much for your time.
Best wishes,
Lily Martin

GLOSSARY
internship (*n*) a period of time that a young person works in a company to get experience in a job

C Rewrite the email below with capital letters in the correct places.

dear ms. ali,
my name is amanda barron. i work with my sister at first city bank in salvador. now i would like a new job.
can we meet on tuesday and talk about your company?
sincerely,
amanda barron

✍ WRITE IT

D Think of a situation and write a formal email to someone you don't know. Include a connection to someone you both know and the reason for writing. Look at the examples in this lesson for help.

E **PAIR WORK** Exchange emails with another student. Write a reply.

REGISTER CHECK

In formal writing, don't write *I want …*

A polite way to say what you want is *I would like …*

Register check

INSIGHT
Teachers report that their students often struggle to master the differences between written and spoken English.

CONTENT
Register check draws on research into the Cambridge English Corpus and highlights potential problem areas for learners.

RESULT
Students transition confidently between written and spoken English and recognize different levels of formality as well as when to use them appropriately.

You spoke. We listened.

Students told us that speaking is the most important skill for them to master, while teachers told us that finding speaking activities which engage their students and work in the classroom can be challenging.

That's why EVOLVE has a whole lesson dedicated to speaking: Lesson 5, *Time to speak*.

Time to speak

INSIGHT

Speaking ability is how students most commonly measure their own progress, but is also the area where they feel most insecure. To be able to fully exploit speaking opportunities in the classroom, students need a safe speaking environment where they can feel confident, supported, and able to experiment with language.

CONTENT

Time to Speak is a unique lesson dedicated to developing speaking skills and is based around immersive tasks which involve information sharing and decision making.

RESULT

Time to speak lessons create a buzz in the classroom where speaking can really thrive, evolve, and take off, resulting in more confident speakers of English.

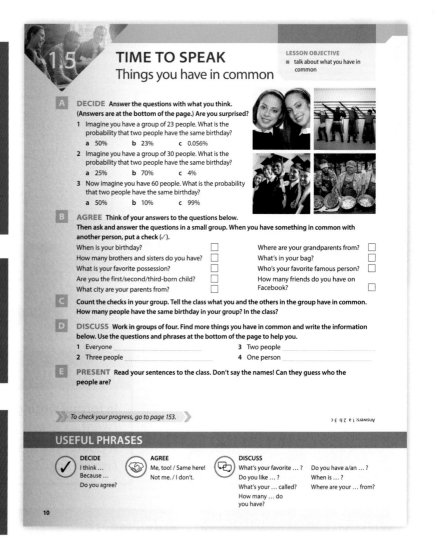

Experience Better Learning with EVOLVE: a course that helps both teachers and students on every step of the language learning journey.

Speaking matters. Find out more about creating safe speaking environments in the classroom.

EVOLVE unit structure

Unit opening page

Each unit opening page activates prior knowledge and vocabulary and immediately gets students speaking.

Lessons 1 and 2

These lessons present and practice the unit vocabulary and grammar in context, helping students discover language rules for themselves. Students then have the opportunity to use this language in well-scaffolded, personalized speaking tasks.

Lesson 3

This lesson is built around a functional language dialogue that models and contextualizes useful fixed expressions for managing a particular situation. This is a real world strategy to help students handle unexpected conversational turns.

Lesson 4

This is a combined skills lesson based around an engaging reading or listening text. Each lesson asks students to think critically and ends with a practical writing task.

Lesson 5

Time to speak is an entire lesson dedicated to developing speaking skills. Students work on collaborative, immersive tasks which involve information sharing and decision making.

CONTENTS

Functional language	Listening	Reading	Writing	Speaking
■ Greet someone for the first time; greet someone who you know; start conversations **Real-world strategy** ■ Show interest and surprise		**Email introductions** ■ Read and correct an email	**A work email** ■ A formal email to someone you don't know ■ Punctuation: capital letters	■ Talk about people you know ■ Ask and answer questions about people in your life ■ Talk about things you have in your bag ■ Say *hello* and start a conversation **Time to speak** ■ Talk about things in common
■ Explain, check, and solve a technology problem **Real-world strategy** ■ Ask for repetition	**How to be successful** ■ A podcast about what successful people do		**A short post on a website** ■ A comment on a website post ■ Use examples and opinions to add interest	■ Talk about your busy life ■ Talk about what you do every day, etc. ■ Talk about work spaces ■ Talk on the phone/online **Time to speak** ■ Talk about apps for work or study
■ Ask for information **Real-world strategy** ■ Check information	**Bike sharing** ■ A report about cycling in Mexico City		**A short social media message** ■ A message to a bike sharing program ■ *and, but,* and *so*	■ Talk about sports that are popular in your country ■ Describe who you see ■ Describe exercise routines ■ Ask for information about a swimming pool **Time to speak** ■ Talk about fitness programs
■ Make and accept invitations; plan where and when to meet **Real-world strategy** ■ Give general excuses	**Waiting for something special** ■ A news report about an unusual event		**An invitation to an event** ■ An event announcement ■ *too, also,* and *as well*	■ Talk about celebrations in your country ■ Arrange to meet after English class ■ Choose gifts ■ Invite someone to an event **Time to speak** ■ Talk about gifts for a trip
■ React to good and bad news **Real-world strategy** ■ Check your understanding		**First impressions** ■ Posts about experiences in a new place	**Online comments** ■ A comment on a message board ■ Agree and disagree	■ Talk about a special picture of you as a child ■ Talk about a special day in your life ■ Ask and answer questions about last weekend ■ Respond to good and bad news **Time to speak** ■ Talk about a famous event in the past
■ Explain your language problem; explain the function of the thing you want **Real-world strategy** ■ Ask for words in English	**Money lessons** ■ Stories about money problems		**Top tips to save money** ■ A vlog script with suggestions for saving money ■ Using referencing: *one* and *them*	■ Talk about where you shop ■ Plan a shopping trip ■ Talk about shopping habits ■ Explain what you want **Time to speak** ■ Present a new invention

CLASSROOM LANGUAGE

◀)) **1.02** **Asking for help**

How do you say that in English?

What does _____ mean?

How do you spell _____ ?

How do you pronounce this word?

Sorry, can you repeat that, please?

Sorry, I don't understand.

Working in pairs and groups

Who wants to start?

Who wants to go first?

Whose turn is it?

It's my turn.

It's your turn.

OK. What do you have for number 1?

Let's compare answers.

UNIT OBJECTIVES
- talk about the people in your life
- talk about possessions
- greet people and start a conversation
- introduce yourself in an email
- talk about what you have in common

START SPEAKING

A   **Look at the picture. What is the connection between the people? What are some different ways people are connected? Read the list and add two more.**

     family   friends   work/school _____

FIND IT

B   **Think about a famous actor in your country: how many connections do you have between you and him/her? You can use your phone to help you.**

C   **Are you a very social person in general? Do you have connections with a lot of different people? For ideas, watch Alessandra's video.**

REAL STUDENT

Are you the same as Alessandra?

1.1 WE'RE FAMILY

LESSON OBJECTIVE
■ talk about the people in your life

1 VOCABULARY: Describing people you know

A ◀))) **1.03** **Look at the pictures. Listen and say the words. Who do you see every day?**

1 neighbors 2 classmates 3 close friends 4 couple / girlfriend / boyfriend
5 boss 6 grandchildren / grandson / granddaughter 7 roommates

B ▶ Now do the vocabulary exercises for 1.1 on page 141.

C PAIR WORK Make five true sentences with five words from exercise 1A. Tell your partner.

2 LANGUAGE IN CONTEXT

A **Look at the picture of Cecilia. Who are the people in her life? Who's in her family? Check (✓) the boxes.**

These are my **classmates**. That's Kiko and Luis on the left. They're from different countries, but we all study English.

This is Marta. We're **close friends**. She's a student in Puebla.

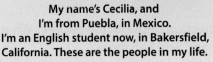
My name's Cecilia, and I'm from Puebla, in Mexico. I'm an English student now, in Bakersfield, California. These are the people in my life.

Here are my brother and sister. Their names are Jose Luis and Yvonne. This is an old photo.

I have more than 200 friends on Facebook, but they're not close friends. Many people are coworkers or school friends.

People always ask, "Is he your **boyfriend**?" No, he's not! He's my **neighbor**, Marcos, and he's a friend.

B **Match the names with their connection to Cecilia.**

1 Yvonne   a neighbor
2 Marta   b close friend
3 Kiko and Luis   c sister
4 Jose Luis   d classmates
5 Marcos   e brother

3 GRAMMAR: *be*; possessive adjectives

A **Complete the rules below. Use the sentences in the grammar box to help you.**

1 *I'm from Puebla.* I'm = _____I am_____

2 *They're not close friends.*
You can also say: *They* _____
close friends.

3 *Is he your boyfriend?*
To answer, you can say:
Yes, he is. or *No, he* _____ .

> **be**
>
> | | | |
> |---|---|---|
> | **I'm** from Puebla. | **I'm not** from Bakersfield. | **Am I** late? |
> | **She's** a student in Puebla. | **He's not** my boyfriend. | **Is he** your classmate? |
> | **We're** close friends. | **They're not** close friends. | **Are you** my new neighbor? |

B **Complete the spaces with the correct possessive adjective. Use the sentences in the grammar box to help you.**

I _____my_____ , you _____ , he _____ , she _____ ,
it _____ .
we _____ , they _____ .

> **Possessive adjectives**
>
> | | | |
> |---|---|---|
> | He's **my** brother. | **His** name's Jose Luis. | They are **our** neighbors. |
> | What's **your** name? | **Her** name's Marta. | He is **their** son. |
> | | The dog hurt **its** foot. | |

C ▶ **Now go to page 129. Look at the grammar chart and do the grammar exercise for 1.1.**

Now go to page 129. Look at the grammar chart and do the grammar exercise for 1.1.

D GROUP WORK **Use the words to write questions. Then read the Accuracy check box and check your work. Use the questions to find out more about your classmates.**

1 his / what's / name / ?   *What's his name?*
2 from / is / where / she / ? _____
3 is / name / her / Maria / ? _____
4 they / from / are / Argentina / ? _____
5 our / is / teacher / American / ? _____
6 are / from / where / parents / your / ? _____

> ✓ **ACCURACY** CHECK
>
> Possessive adjectives agree with the possessor.
> This is a photo of my wife with ~~their~~ parents. ✗
> This is a photo of my wife with her parents. ✓

4 SPEAKING

A **Look at the picture of Cecilia and her connections on page 2. Make a similar picture for your life. Write the names of your connections. Watch Seung Geyoung's video.**

REAL STUDENT
What family members does she say? Are they the same as your family?

B PAIR WORK **Ask and answer questions about your pictures. You can show photos of the people on your phone.**

FIND IT

Who is Rogelio? | He's a coworker at my office.

Are Bob and Vera your parents? | Yes, they are.

WHAT'S IN YOUR BAG?

1 VOCABULARY: Naming everyday things

A ◀)) **1.04** **Look at the pictures. Listen and say the words. Do you have these things in your bag?**

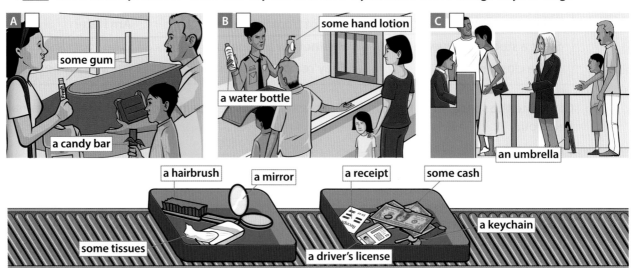

A
some gum
a candy bar

B
some hand lotion
a water bottle

C
an umbrella

a hairbrush a mirror a receipt some cash
a keychain
some tissues a driver's license

B ▶ **Now do the vocabulary exercises for 1.2 on page 141.**

C PAIR WORK **Choose an item from exercise 1A. Your partner asks you questions to guess the item.**

Is it a mirror? Yes, it is.

Are they tissues? No, they aren't.

2 LANGUAGE IN CONTEXT

A ◀)) **1.05** **Look at the pictures in exercise 1A again. Where are the people? Listen to the conversations and match them to the pictures.**

◀)) **1.05 Audio script**

1 A Is that your umbrella?

B No, it's not mine. I think it belongs to those people. Perhaps it's theirs.

A Hmm. Excuse me, is this yours?

C Oh, yes! Thanks. That's my wife's umbrella.

D Thanks so much!

2 A Excuse me! Whose is this?

B It's not ours. I think it's hers – the woman with the little girl there.

A Excuse me, ma'am. Is this yours?

C What? Oh, yes, that's mine.

A I'm sorry, but you can't take hand lotion and a water bottle on the plane.

C But they're my daughter's. She needs them!

3 A I think that's my grandson's bag.

B No, sorry, it isn't his. It's mine. It belongs to me. Look, there's my pack of gum.

A You're right. So where's my grandson's bag?

B There's another blue one. Is that one his?

B 🔊 **1.05** **Listen again and read. Match the items with their owners.**

1 The water bottle ☐ 2 The umbrella ☐ 3 The blue bag ☐

3 GRAMMAR: Possession

A (Circle) **the correct answers. Use the sentences in the grammar box to help you.**

1 Which response is <u>not</u> correct: *Whose is this?*
   a *It's mine.*   c *It's my grandson's bag.*
   b *It's black.*   d *It belongs to me.*

2 What comes after *my?*
   a a noun   b nothing

3 What comes after *mine?*
   a a noun   b nothing

4 What does the *'s* in *my grandson's bag* mean?
   a *is*   b it shows possession

Possession
That's **my** grandson's bag. **Whose** water bottle is this?
No, sorry. It isn't **his**. It's **mine**. It's not **ours**. I think it's **hers**.
It **belongs to** me.

B PAIR WORK **Look at exercise 2B above again.**
   Make sentences with *belong to* for each item and its owner(s).
   The water bottle belongs to …

C ▶ **Now go to page 129. Look at the grammar chart and do the grammar exercise for 1.2.**

D **Complete the conversations with the correct possessive form of the word in parentheses. Practice the conversations with a partner.**

1 A ¹____Whose____ (who) water bottle is
     this?
   B It isn't ²_____ (I). Maybe it's
     ³_____ (he).

2 A Sorry, which bag is ⁴_____ (I)?
   B That one is ⁵_____ (you). And
     the other ones are ⁶_____
     (they).

4 SPEAKING

GROUP WORK **Choose three things from your pockets or bags and put them all together on one desk. Who do the different things belong to? Use possessives instead of names.**

OK, so, I think the tissues are yours.   Right! Whose mirror is this? Is it your mirror?

1.3 HOW DO YOU KNOW RAQUEL?

1 FUNCTIONAL LANGUAGE

A 🔊 1.06 **Look at the pictures. What is the connection between the people? Listen to the conversations and match them to the pictures. Are you right?**

A ☐

B ☐

🔊 **1.06 Audio script**

1 A Good morning! Are you Robert?
  B Yes, I am.
  A **Pleased to meet you**. I'm Julie, your coworker here.
  B **Great to meet you, too**.
  A I'm here to help. This is your desk, right here.
  B Oh, OK. This is a nice office.
  A **Do you know anybody here?**
  B No, I don't.

2 A Hey, Raquel!
  B Simon! **Long time**, **no see**! Please come in.
  A **Great to see you again**!
  B **It's really good to see you**.
  B Oh, here's Patrick! Patrick, meet Simon.
  A Hello, Patrick. **How do you know Raquel? Are you a friend of hers?**
  C I'm her husband.

B **Complete the chart with expressions in bold from the conversations above.**

Greeting someone for the first time	Greeting someone who you know	Starting conversations
Good morning. Are you (Robert)?	Long time, [3]_____ _____ !	Do you [6]_____ anybody here?
Pleased to [1]_____ _____ .	[4]_____ to see you again!	[7]_____ do you know (Raquel)?
Great to meet you, [2]_____ .	It's really [5]_____ to see you.	Are you a [8]_____ of hers / his / theirs?

C ⬚ PAIR WORK **Greet your partner. Now change partners. Imagine you don't know your new partner, and greet them.**

6

SHOWING INTEREST AND SURPRISE
You can use some common expressions to show interest and surprise.
Wow!   Seriously?
Is it really? / Are you really?

A 🔊 **1.07** **Read about showing interest and surprise in the box above. Use the expressions there to complete the conversation below. Listen to the full conversation and check.**

A Do you know anybody here?
B No, I don't. I'm pretty new to this city, too.
A ¹ _____? A new city *and* a new job – that's a lot! Well, that's Mr. Patel. He's the boss. His office is across from your desk.
B ² _____? That's good to know.

> **INSIDER ENGLISH**
>
> ***pretty*** = *beautiful*
> *That's a **pretty** little house.*
> ***pretty*** + **adjective** = *very*
> *That's **pretty** good. (**That's very good.**)*

B PAIR WORK **Practice the conversation from exercise 2A, above.**

3 PRONUNCIATION: Saying /l/ at the end of a word

A 🔊 **1.08** **Listen. Focus on the /l/ sounds. Practice saying the words.**

1 You look wonder**ful**.   2 Beauti**ful** weather, isn't it?   3 How do you know Rach**el**?

B 🔊 **1.09** **Listen. Who pronounces the /l/ sound at the end of the words clearly? Write A or B.**

1 beautiful *B*   3 full ____   5 people ____
2 bottle ____   4 girl ____   6 couple ____

C PAIR WORK **Say the words in exercise B to your partner. Does your partner say the /l/ sound?**

4 SPEAKING

A PAIR WORK **Read the situations. Then put the conversations in order. Read them with a partner.**

Situation 1: You're at a conference. Greet people you don't know.
- [ ] Good to meet you, too. Do you know anybody here?
- [ ] I'm Diana Reyes. Great to meet you.
- [ ] No, it's my first time at this conference.
- [1] Hello. I'm Daniel Santiago.

Situation 2: You arrive at a coffee shop to meet people you know.
- [ ] I know! Great to see you again!
- [1] Hi, Akram.
- [ ] Yeah, you, too. Hey, this is a nice place.
- [ ] Hi, Lola. Long time, no see!
- [ ] Yeah, isn't it?

B **Choose one of the conversations and add more to it. Use the language from this lesson. Then act out your conversation for the class.**

1.4 EMAIL INTRODUCTIONS

1 READING

A **PAIR WORK** How many emails do you write in a month? Why do you write them? Do you write emails in English? Tell your partner.

B **READ FOR MAIN IDEAS** Read the email and choose the main idea.

- ☐ He wants a job.
- ☐ He wants information about food.
- ☐ He wants cooking lessons.

C **READ FOR DETAIL** There are problems with Chris's email. Read the comments (A–F) and match them with the correct part of the email.

A What is your email about? You need a subject!

B Begin a formal sentence with *Dear Ms. / Mrs. / Mr. (last name)* or just *Dear Hiring Manager* or *Dear (job title)*. It's not a good idea to begin with *Hello, Hi,* or *Dear Friend*. You're not a friend!

C End the email with *Best wishes* or *All the best* and write your full name.

D A funny email address is OK for friends but not for people you don't know.

E Check your writing before you send your email.

F Don't use emojis in a formal email.

D Read the Register check box and correct the problem in Chris's email.

E 🔊 **1.10** **PAIR WORK** **THINK CRITICALLY** Listen to Dave's response to Chris's email. Does Dave offer Chris a job? Why not? What research do you need to do before you ask someone for a job? Discuss with your partner.

REGISTER CHECK

In formal writing, don't write *I want …*

A polite way to say what you want is *I would like …*

2 WRITING

A Read the email. Does the writer follow the advice from the comments on page 8?

To: r.johnson65@listmail.net
From: lilymartin@mymail.org
Subject: Internship – Lily Martin

B **WRITING SKILLS** Look at the email again and (circle) the capital letters. Write the words with capital letters.

a pronoun (*I, you, he, she*, etc.)   I

b the beginning of a sentence

c names (people and organizations)

d titles (*Mr., Dr., Prof.*)

e places (countries, nationalities, towns)

f days of the week, months

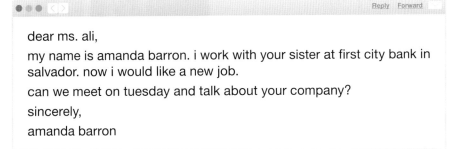

Dear Mr. Johnson,

Your daughter Abigail is my classmate at the University of Toronto.

In October and November every year, students in our class do an **internship**. I would like to do an internship in your company, Grallen Technologies. I attach my résumé to this email.

Thank you very much for your time.

Best wishes,

Lily Martin

GLOSSARY

internship (*n*) a period of time that a young person works in a company to get experience in a job

C Rewrite the email below with capital letters in the correct places.

Reply Forward

dear ms. ali,

my name is amanda barron. i work with your sister at first city bank in salvador. now i would like a new job.

can we meet on tuesday and talk about your company?

sincerely,

amanda barron

WRITE IT

D Think of a situation and write a formal email to someone you don't know. Include a connection to someone you both know and the reason for writing. Look at the examples in this lesson for help.

E PAIR WORK Exchange emails with another student. Write a reply.

TIME TO SPEAK
Things you have in common

A **DECIDE** Answer the questions with what you think. (Answers are at the bottom of the page.) Are you surprised?

1 Imagine you have a group of 23 people. What is the probability that two people have the same birthday?

a 50%   b 23%   c 0.056%

2 Imagine you have a group of 30 people. What is the probability that two people have the same birthday?

a 25%   b 70%   c 4%

3 Now imagine you have 60 people. What is the probability that two people have the same birthday?

a 50%   b 10%   c 99%

B **AGREE** Think of your answers to the questions below. Then ask and answer the questions in a small group. When you have something in common with another person, put a check (✓).

When is your birthday? ☐

How many brothers and sisters do you have? ☐

What is your favorite possession? ☐

Are you the first/second/third-born child? ☐

What city are your parents from? ☐

Where are your grandparents from? ☐

What's in your bag? ☐

Who's your favorite famous person? ☐

How many friends do you have on Facebook? ☐

C Count the checks in your group. Tell the class what you and the others in the group have in common. How many people have the same birthday in your group? In the class?

D **DISCUSS** Work in groups of four. Find more things you have in common and write the information below. Use the questions and phrases at the bottom of the page to help you.

1 Everyone _____

2 Three people _____

3 Two people _____

4 One person _____

E **PRESENT** Read your sentences to the class. Don't say the names! Can they guess who the people are?

To check your progress, go to page 153.

Answers: 1 a 2 b 3 c

USEFUL PHRASES

 DECIDE
I think …
Because …
Do you agree?

 AGREE
Me, too! / Same here!
Not me. / I don't.

 DISCUSS
What's your favorite … ?
Do you like … ?
What's your … called?
How many … do you have?

Do you have a/an … ?
When is … ?
Where are your … from?

WORK AND STUDY

2

UNIT OBJECTIVES

- talk about what you do every day, on the weekend, etc.
- talk about your workspace
- explain communication problems
- write your opinion about a podcast
- give advice about useful apps for work and study

Notifications ▾

6:30 a.m.
Morning alarm

8:00 p.m.
Dinner with Mom
at 17 Elm Street

30 minutes ago
5 new emails

START SPEAKING

A   Look at the picture. Who are the people? Where are they?

B   Are you a very busy person? How do you remember all your plans? For example, do you use the calendar on your phone or do you write them down?

C   Is this a busy week for you? Watch Allison's video.

REAL STUDENT

Is your busy day the same as Allison's?

2.1 KNOW YOUR NUMBERS

1 LANGUAGE IN CONTEXT

A **Julia has a new fitness tracker. Read the article. Check (✓) the things it gives her information about.**

- ☐ class schedule
- ☐ drinking
- ☐ eating
- ☐ exercise
- ☐ free-time activities
- ☐ sleep
- ☐ study time
- ☐ the weather
- ☐ work

My life in **NUMBERS**

What do I know about my life?
A lot more with my new **fitness tracker**.

Now I know I take 7,000 steps a day – not bad, but not great. But I also know that I look at my laptop for 10.5 hours every day! About 78% of that time (8.2 hours) is for work. When I have free time, I chat with friends (64 messages a day) or make plans for later.

I only sleep six hours a night (25%). Then I have something to drink (coffee or soda) about eight times a day to stay awake. Thank you, caffeine!!

The good news? I exercise a lot because I do a lot of housework (my roommate doesn't do anything). I do the laundry, the cooking, and the dishes, and I make the bed. That's about the same as walking 7.5 kilometers a day!

Learn your numbers with a **fitness tracker**! It can teach you a lot about you!

fitness tracker

GLOSSARY
step (*n*) a movement you make with your feet when you walk

B **Read Julia's article again. Does Julia need extra exercise? Why or why not?**

C **Do you think information like this is useful? Why or why not?**

2 VOCABULARY: Expressions with *do*, *have*, and *make*

A 🔊 **1.11** **Listen and say the phrases. How many of these phrases are in the article?**

DO
- the dishes
- the laundry
- the housework
- some work

HAVE
- a party
- free time
- a snack
- something to drink

MAKE
- the bed
- plans

Dinner at Amy's, 7pm

B ▶ **Now do the vocabulary exercises for 2.1 on page 142.**

12

C PAIR WORK Which activities in exercise 2A do you usually do every day? Do you and your partner do the same things? Watch Celeste's video.

REAL STUDENT

Do you do the same activities as Celeste?

3 GRAMMAR: Simple present for habits and routines

A **Complete the rules below. Use the sentences in the grammar box to help you.**

1 In affirmative sentences, add the letter _____ to the verb when you talk about *he/she/it*.

2 In negative sentences, use *I don't* and *you don't*, but *he* or *she* _____ .

3 For questions, add the letters _____ to *do* when you ask about *he/she/it*.

4 For information questions, the question word (*what, when, where, who, why, how*) is before *do* or _____ .

Simple present for habits and routines

I **do** the laundry and the cooking   My roommate **doesn't do** anything.   **Do** you **do** the laundry?
Julia **sleeps** six hours a night.   Julia **doesn't need** more exercise.   **Does** Julia **sleep** a lot?

Information questions

What does Julia **know** about her life?
How many steps do you **take** every day?
How often do you **have** something to drink?

B ▶ **Now go to page 130. Look at the grammar chart and do the grammar exercise for 2.1.**

C **Put the words in the right order to make questions and answers. Then check your accuracy.**

1 A day / does / start / usually / When / your
   B at / It / starts / usually / 7:00 a.m.

2 A coffees / day / do / every / have / How / many / you
   B cups / day / every / four / have / I

3 A dishes / do / do / How / often / the / you
   B dishes / do / evening / every / I / the

4 A does / family / dinner / have / time / What / your
   B at / eat / seven / usually / We

5 A do / hours / How / many / sleep / you
   B always / for / hours / I / seven / sleep

✓ **ACCURACY** CHECK

Put these frequency words before the verb:
usually, often, never, sometimes

Put other time phrases at the end of the sentence: *every day, every evening*

I do housework ~~usually~~ on Saturdays. ✗
I usually do housework on Saturdays. ✓

---

4 SPEAKING

PAIR WORK Ask and answer the five questions from exercise 3C. Give answers that are true for you.

13

2.2 WHERE'S YOUR WORKSPACE?

1 VOCABULARY: Naming work and study items

A Do you usually use pen and paper, a computer, your phone, or a tablet at work or school? Why?

B 🔊 **1.12** Look at the pictures. Listen and say the words. Which things do you use every day?

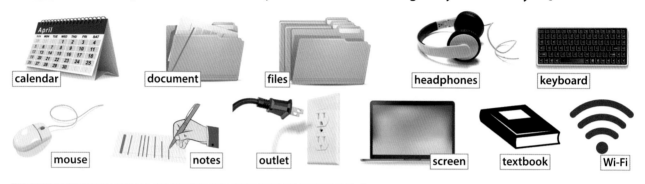

calendar   document   files   headphones   keyboard

mouse   notes   outlet   screen   textbook   Wi-Fi

C ▶ Now do the vocabulary exercises for 2.2 on page 142.

2 LANGUAGE IN CONTEXT

A Where do you like to work or study? Choose from these places. Why do you like to work or study there?

at home   at school   in a café   in a library   in a park   in an office

B 🔊 **1.13** Listen to three people talk about their favorite workspaces. Match the speakers to the pictures. Listen again and read to check.

🔊 1.13 Audio script

1 This is my office. Well, kind of. There are lots of tables here. These small ones on the left are my favorite. I often have meetings in here, and there's lots of space to sit and see the same **screen**. There's free **Wi-Fi**, and the coffee is excellent, too!

2 Where do I work? In the spring and summer, I like to sit under these trees. All my **notes** and **files** and **textbooks** are on my laptop, so I don't need anything else. That's a mall over there, so I can have something to drink or a snack when I want.

3 This is where I usually study. I live a long way from school, so I'm here for two hours every day. Do you see that seat with the table, on the left? That's my favorite one. It's always quiet – I listen to music with my **headphones**. There's an electrical **outlet** between the seats.

A

B

C

C PAIR WORK Discuss the workspaces in the pictures. What's good and bad about them? Are these places better than the other places in exercise 2A? Why or why not?

3 GRAMMAR: *This / that one; these / those ones*

A Look at the pictures and complete the sentences with *this one*, *that one*, *these ones*, or *those ones*.

1 _____

_____ are my favorites.

2 I like _____

_____ in the corner.

3 _____

_____ are very small.

4 _____

_____ has an electrical outlet.

B Complete the rules with *one* or *ones*.

1 Use *this* or *that* _____ to talk about a singular thing that is near (*this*) or far (*that*).

2 Use *these* or *those* _____ to talk about plural things that are near (*these*) or far (*those*).

> **!**
> Use *this*, *that*, *these*, and *those* with or without a noun.
>
> *This **table**'s my favorite. **This** is my favorite table.*
>
> ***One*** and ***ones*** replace a noun.
>
> *This **table**'s my favorite. This **one**'s my favorite.*

C ▶ **Now go to page 131. Do the grammar exercise for 2.2.**

D Look at the picture and complete the conversation with *this*, *that*, *these*, *those*, *one*, or *ones*.

A Is ¹ ___this___ a drawing of your office?

B Yes, it is. ² _____ is my desk here, in the corner.

A What's ³ _____ green thing here? And what are ⁴ _____ ones on the round table there?

B This green one is my chair, and those ⁵ _____ are more chairs.

A And ⁶ _____ things on your desk, what are they?

B ⁷ _____ are my files and documents. And those ⁸ _____ there on the table are more files.

A And what's ⁹ _____ pink thing there?

B A place for books. Books I never look at!

4 SPEAKING

A PAIR WORK Draw <u>your</u> usual work or study space. Ask and answer questions about it with your partner. Use the questions in the box.

Where is this?	What's this here?	What's that over there?	What's that one?
Where is that?	What's this/that?	What are those/these?	Is this/that your laptop?

> OK, so where's this?

> This is where I usually work.

> Is that your desk there?

> No, this one's my desk, here. And that's my laptop.

B GROUP WORK **What do you like about your workspace and your partner's workspace? What don't you like? Tell your group.**

2.3 THE CONNECTION'S TERRIBLE

LESSON OBJECTIVE
■ explain communication problems

1 FUNCTIONAL LANGUAGE

A 🔊 **1.14** Look at the communication problems in the box. Can you think of any more? Read and listen to the conversations. What communication problems do they have?

| a bad connection | no battery | no picture | problems hearing | someone speaking too fast |

🔊 1.14 Audio script

1
A Hi, Hannah.
B Hi there, Pedro. How are you?
A Can you say that again? I can see you, but I **can't hear you very well.**
B Really? That's strange, I can hear you just fine, but I can't see you.
A Sorry, I lost you. What was that?
B I can't see you.
A Maybe **it's my Wi-Fi. Is that any better?**
B No, **the connection's terrible. We can try again later.**
A Fine, let's do that. Talk to you later.

2
A Hi, Hannah. **Can you hear me now?**
B Sorry, **you're breaking up.** Pedro, **are you still there?**
A Yes, still here, … but **there's an echo** now.
B Uh, … OK, wait. **Let me turn up the volume. How about now?**
A No, no better, sorry.
B **Let me call you,** OK?
A What? I didn't catch that.
B Let me call you.
A No, still nothing. I know! Let me call you.

B Complete the chart with the expressions in **bold** from the conversations above.

INSIDER ENGLISH

When you can't hear someone because of a bad connection, you *lose* them.
*Sorry, I **lost** you.   I **lost** you there for a few seconds.*

Explaining the problem	Checking the problem	Solving the problem
I can't hear you very well.	Is that any better?	We can try again later.
It's my ¹_____ .	Can you ⁵_____ me now?	Let me turn up the ⁸_____ .
The ²_____ 's terrible.	How ⁶_____ ?	Let me ⁹_____ , OK?
You're ³_____ .	Are you ⁷_____ ?	
There's an ⁴_____ now.		

C **PAIR WORK** Practice the conversations in exercise 1A with your partner.

2 REAL-WORLD STRATEGY

ASKING FOR REPETITION
Use these expressions when you can't hear or understand what someone says.

Sorry, can you say that again?   *What? I didn't catch that.*

Could you repeat that?

A   Read the expressions in the box above. Find one more example on page 16 and add it to the box.

B   🔊 **1.15** Complete the conversations using the expressions in the box. Then listen and check. Practice them with a partner.

A

A   Sorry, I lost you. Can you
    1_____ ?

B   Yes, it's the hotel's Wi-Fi – it's terrible!

A   Sorry, I ² _____ .

B   The hotel Wi-Fi is terrible!

B

A   Sorry, ³_____ that?
    The traffic noise is terrible.

B   I said, "I'm running out of battery."

A   Oh, OK. We can try again later.

3 PRONUNCIATION: Saying /h/ at the beginning of a word

A   🔊 **1.16** Listen. Write the missing words. Which sound do they all have?

A   ¹_____ there, Pedro. ²_____ are you?

B   ³_____ , ⁴_____ . Can you ⁵_____ me now?

B   🔊 **1.17** Listen. (Circle) the words you hear.

1 Hi! / eye	3 how / Ow!	5 his / is	7 Hannah / Anna
2 hear / ear	4 head / Ed	6 hate / eight	8 hat / at

C   🔊 **1.18** Listen and repeat. Focus on the /h/ sounds.

1   I can't **h**ear you. The **h**otel's Wi-Fi is terrible.

2   I **h**ave **h**eadphones at **h**ome.

3   Can you **h**ear me OK? **H**ow about now?

4   I **h**ate **h**ousework!

4 SPEAKING

▶ PAIR WORK   Choose a situation with your partner. Student A: Go to page 157.
Student B: Go to page 159. Follow the instructions.

Situations

■ worker (A) to boss (B)   ■ coworker (A) to coworker (B)

■ student (A) to student (B)   ■ student (A) to teacher (B)

HOW TO BE SUCCESSFUL

LESSON OBJECTIVE
■ write your opinion about a podcast

1 LISTENING

A **Look at the title of the book. What are the habits of effective people, do you think? Here are some ideas.**

- ☐ clothes
- ☐ hobbies, interests, and sports
- ☐ food and drink
- ☐ ways of thinking
- ☐ sleeping habits

B ◀)) **1.19** **LISTEN FOR GIST** **Listen to a podcast about the ideas in the book. Put the topics in exercise 1A in the order you hear them (1–4). There is one topic that isn't in the podcast.**

C ◀)) **1.19** **LISTEN FOR DETAILS** **Listen to the podcast again and match the names to what the people usually do.**

1 Sergey Brin ____
2 Warren Buffett ____
3 Tim Cook ____
4 Seth Godin ____
5 Sheryl Sandberg ____

FIND IT

D ◀)) **1.20** **PAIR WORK** **What do you know about the people in exercise 1C? Where do they work, or how do they make money? Discuss with a partner. You can go online to find out more. Listen and check your ideas.**

E **PAIR WORK** **THINK CRITICALLY** **Answer the questions.**

1 Is it a good idea to copy the habits of successful people? Why or why not?
2 Why do you think *The 7 Habits of Highly Effective People* and similar books are so popular? Who do you think buys these books?

2 PRONUNCIATION: Listening for contractions

A ◀)) **1.21** **Listen. Write the missing letters.**

1 **There'**___ a book called *The 7 Habits of Highly Effective People*.
2 **Can'**___ you tell us what they do?
3 They **don'**___ wear normal clothes.

B ◀)) **1.22** **Complete the sentences with the three bold words from exercise 2A. Listen and check.**

1 _____ has the same vowel sound as *coat*.
2 _____ often sounds stronger than *can*.
3 _____ often comes before *a* or *an*. The /z/ sound at the end connects to *a*.

3 WRITING

A **Read the comments about the podcast. Then (circle) (A, B, or C).**

1 A B C   does not think that we can learn a lot from people's daily routines.

2 A B C   gives information about the daily routine of another successful person.

3 A B C   wants information about the daily routine of another successful person.

🎧 PODCAST CHAT
                                                                       ⓐ Profile   ⓢ Log out

[A] **The podcast is very interesting**, but why are all these examples of businesspeople in America? There are other successful people – people from other countries, artists and creative people, more women. I would like to know about Viviane Senna, **for example**. What does she do every day on a normal day? We never read about her personal life.

[B] Warren Buffett plays the ukulele? Give me a break! This is NOT a reason for his success. **I don't believe** we can learn anything from this information. The only important thing is the way people think.

[C] **Another example is** Jack Dorsey of Twitter. He does the same things every day. He gets up at 5:00 a.m. and meditates for 30 minutes, exercises, and then has his first coffee. On the weekend, he plays sports, and he thinks about the next week. **Like all the others** in the podcast, he's really successful.

B **WRITING SKILLS** **Look at the phrases in bold in the comments above. Match each phrase to a category.**

1 Giving an opinion _____

2 Giving an example _____

3 Comparing _____

🌐 WRITE IT

C **Write a comment of 40–60 words about the podcast. Use the comments in exercise 3A and the phrases in exercise 3B to help you. You can:**

- Give your opinion of the podcast.
- Give an example of the daily routines of a successful person you know.
- Compare one of these successful people to another successful person you know.

D **There are spelling mistakes in some of the words below. Correct the mistakes. Then check your spelling in exercise 3C.**

belive _____   poeple _____

businesspeople _____   personal _____

exercise _____   realy _____

intresting _____   successful _____

E **Read the comments of other students in your class. Choose one comment that you think is interesting and write a short reply.**

TIME TO SPEAK
Apps for life

USE IT

A Look at the different categories of apps on the right. Which ones do you have on your phone? Which ones do you use every day? Why do you like them? Does your partner use the same apps?

B Read what the students say, and give advice on apps useful for them.

> I want to practice English vocab when I'm on the bus to school. I need a fun, interesting app.

Leon

> I always forget what my homework is and when to do it. I need an app that helps me remember.

Susana

> When I take notes in class, my writing is terrible, and the next day, I can't read it. Is there an app I can use to take notes quickly?

Maria

> I'd like to learn more about American culture. I love TV and movies – is there a good app with lots of American shows?

David

C **DISCUSS** Think about what types of apps you would like to help you study English. Discuss in your group. Use the phrases at the bottom of the page to help you.

D **DECIDE** Your school wants to give a "welcome pack" of four smartphone or tablet apps to new students. Choose four apps from your phones and say why they are useful.

E **PRESENT** Tell the class about your group's suggestions. Listen to the other suggestions. Write down any apps that you think are useful for you.

F Tell your partner which apps from today you'd like to download, and why. How are you going to use the apps?

>> *To check your progress, go to page 153.* >>

social media | communication

games | calendar

education | sports and leisure

news | music and podcasts

photos and video | health and fitness

USEFUL PHRASES

DISCUSS
I want to … / I'd like to …
I find it hard to …
Is there an app I can use to … ?
How does it work?
Why do you like it?

DECIDE
My advice is …
Let's choose this app because …

PRESENT
We think this is a great/helpful/fun app.
We like this app because …

UNIT OBJECTIVES

- talk about what you're doing at the moment
- talk about sports and exercise
- ask for information
- write short messages to a company
- create a fitness program

LET'S MOVE

3

START SPEAKING

A   What are the people in the picture doing? Is this a good picture to represent sports?

B   Which big sports events do you like to watch on TV? Why do you like them?

C   How important are sports for you or in your country?
Explain your reasons. For ideas, watch Irene's video.

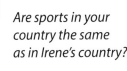

REAL STUDENT

Are sports in your country the same as in Irene's country?

3.1 WE'RE WINNING!

LESSON OBJECTIVE
- talk about what you're doing at the moment

1 VOCABULARY: Sports

A 🔊 1.23 **Look at the pictures. What sports do you see? Work with a partner and match the pictures to the words. Listen and say the words.**

athlete	court	fans	field	goal	gym
lose	~~player~~	pool	race	team	win

1 player
2

3

4

5

6

7

8

9

10

11
12

B **Are the words above (a) events, (b) people, (c) places, or (d) results. Make four lists. Add one more word to each list.**

C ▶ **Now do the vocabulary exercises for 3.1 on page 142.**

D [PAIR WORK] **Which sports do you play? Where do you watch sports?**

2 LANGUAGE IN CONTEXT

A **Read about the action in two sports events: a soccer game ⚽ and a tennis game 🎾. Circle the correct sport in each update.**

SPORTS LIVE

 a) The 45,000 Brazilian and 35,000 Uruguayan **fans** are incredible! They're making a lot of noise. Here come the **players**.

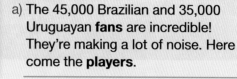 b) Gomez **loses** the first game of this final. It's getting hot here on the **court**: 33°C. The world number one isn't playing well today.

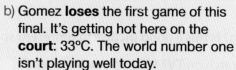 c) 1–0! Fantastic **goal**! Uruguay is **winning**! The Brazilian players can't believe it.

d) Gomez wins the second game, but something's wrong. What's he doing now? He's calling a doctor onto the court.

e) Wait, it's not a goal! No goal! Now the Uruguayan team can't believe it. Everyone is on the **field**. It's crazy!

f) Gomez is leaving the court. He's crying. It's a terrible end to the game for this star **athlete**.

B **Read the SportsLive updates again. In which sport …**

a is a player hurt? _____   b is it a final? _____   c are there lots of people? _____

3 GRAMMAR: Present continuous

A (Circle) the correct option to complete the rule. Use the sentences in the grammar box to help you.

We use the present continuous for actions that happen **usually or all the time / right now.**

> **Present continuous**
>
> It**'s getting** hot here on the court.   What **is** he **doing** now?
>
> The world number one **isn't playing** well today.   Gomez **is leaving** the court.

B ▶ **Now go to page 131. Look at the grammar chart and do the grammar exercise for 3.1.**

C PAIR WORK **What are the fans doing in the picture? Find five things. Tell your partner.**

4 SPEAKING

A **Read the conversation. Why is Kate calling Pedro?**

Pedro Where are you?

Kate I'm in a restaurant. And guess what! Ronaldo is sitting at the table right next to me! Ronaldo!

Pedro Really? What's he doing?

Kate He's eating a sandwich!

Pedro No way! Take a picture.

> **INSIDER** ENGLISH
>
> Say *Guess what!* when you have something interesting or surprising to say, and you want someone to really listen.

B **Imagine you're in a restaurant and you see a famous athlete. Think of answers to these questions.**

> Where are you?   Who can you see?   Who is he/she with?   What are they doing?

C PAIR WORK **Call your partner to tell them about your famous person from exercise 4B. Use the conversation in exercise 4A as a model.**

3.2 THE 16TH STEP

1 LANGUAGE IN CONTEXT

A **Look at the pictures. What sports do you see?**

B 🔊 **1.24 Listen to the podcast. Which picture from exercise 1A are they talking about?**

C 🔊 **1.24 Listen again and read. Why is Lex on the Paralympic team? What does he do that you can't?**

🔊 **1.24 Audio script**

Tyler Do you exercise much?

Bree I **stretch** every morning when I wake up. I **climb** the stairs to come here. And now I'm **lifting** my coffee cup.

Tyler Seriously? Well, today we're talking about a real athlete: Lex Gillette.

Bree I think I know that name.

Tyler Yes. He's amazing! He has four Paralympic silver medals for long jump.

Bree Wow!

Tyler Yeah – and he's blind.

Bree What? You mean he can run and **jump**, but he can't see? How does he do it?

Tyler He practices more than 30 hours a week.

Bree Really? Hey, maybe he's jumping right now!

Tyler I don't think so. It's early, so I think he's probably stretching now. Athletes stretch a lot, and they usually go to the gym and **lift** weights.

Bree But Lex can't see, so how does he do the long jump?

Tyler When he runs, he knows the number of steps to take: 16. On the 16th step, he jumps.

Bree That's scary! But it's awesome!

D [PAIR WORK] **Which sports from exercise 1 do you like to do? Imagine you are blind. Can you do the sports well? What problems does a blind athlete have?**

2 VOCABULARY: Exercising

A 🔊 **1.25** **Listen and say the words. What two activities are the people doing in the pictures on page 24?**

| climb | jump | lie down | lift | push | sit down | stand up | stretch | throw | turn |

B PAIR WORK **Look at the activities. Describe the routine to a partner. For ideas, watch Celeste's video.**

> Stand up. Now stretch your arms.

REAL STUDENT

Whose routine is more difficult? Yours or Celeste's?

C ▶ **Now do the vocabulary exercises for 3.2 on page 143.**

3 GRAMMAR: Simple present and present continuous

A ⟲Circle⟳ **the correct options to complete the rules. Use the sentences in the grammar box to help you.**

Use the simple present when actions happen **usually / at the time of speaking**.

Use the present continuous when actions happen **usually / at the time of speaking**.

Simple present and present continuous

Do you **exercise** much?   I**'m lifting** my coffee cup.

I stretch every morning   He**'s jumping** right now.

✓ **ACCURACY** CHECK

Use the *-ing* form of the verb with the present continuous.

I'm ~~watch~~ the game now. ✗
I'm watching the game now. ✓

B ▶ **Now go to page 132. Do the grammar exercise for 3.2.**

C **Put the verbs in the correct form. Then check your accuracy.**

A I _____'m thinking_____ (think) of a famous soccer player.

B Where ¹_____ (he / come) from?

A He ²_____ (come) from Brazil, but right now he ³_____ (live) in Spain.

B ⁴_____ (he / play) in the game on TV right now?

A No, he ⁵_____ (not be).

D PAIR WORK **Think of a famous athlete, but don't tell your partner. Ask questions to guess your partner's famous athlete.**

4 SPEAKING

A **Think of a friend you know who exercises a lot. Prepare answers to these questions.**

What kind of exercise does he/she do?   How often does he/she exercise or play sports?

Why does he/she like this activity?   What is he/she probably doing right now?

B GROUP WORK **Talk about your friends. Ask and answer the questions in exercise 4A and think of three more questions.**

COULD YOU TELL ME … ?

1 FUNCTIONAL LANGUAGE

A **Look at the pictures. What places do you see?**

B 🔊 **1.26** **Read and listen. In conversation 1, why doesn't the police officer know where he can buy a T-shirt? In conversation 2, do you think the man buys the T-shirt? Why or why not?**

🔊 **1.26 Audio script**

1 A Excuse me. **We're looking for** section C.
   B Section C is … over there, I think.
   A Thanks. **Do you know** when the game starts?
   B Seven-thirty.
   A Great. One more thing. **Could you tell me** where I can get a T-shirt?
   B I'm not sure. I don't work here. Try the store.
   A OK. Thank you.

2 A Excuse me. **I'm looking for** a large T-shirt.
   B All the T-shirts are over there. The large shirts are on the right.
   A I see them, thanks. Um, **do you know** the price of this white shirt? There's no price tag.
   B Sure. This one is $55.
   A Oh! OK, thank you.

C **Complete the chart with expressions in bold from the conversations above.**

Asking for information

Excuse me.
We're ¹_____ (section C).
I'm ²_____ (a large T-shirt).
Could ³_____ where I can get (a T-shirt)?
Do ⁴_____ (when the game starts)?
Do ⁵_____ (the price of this white shirt)?

D 🔊 **1.27** **Complete the conversations. Then listen and check. Practice with a partner.**

1 A Excuse me. *Could you tell me / I'm looking for* what time the gym closes?   B At nine-thirty.
2 A *I'm looking for / Do you know* the way to court number three?   B Sure. It's over there.

2 REAL-WORLD STRATEGY

A 🔊 **1.28** Listen to another conversation in the store. What information does the woman ask for?

B 🔊 **1.28** Listen again and (circle) what the woman does when she doesn't understand.

   a She repeats his words as a question.   **b** She tells him she doesn't understand.

> **CHECKING INFORMATION**
>
> To check information you don't understand, you can repeat words as questions.
>
> *Do you want a bag for that? They're* **five cents**.
>
> *Sorry?* **Five cents**?
>
> *The bag, for the T-shirt. It's* **five cents**.

C 🔊 **1.29** Read about checking information in the box. Then listen to the questions and respond after the beep to check information.

   1 A Could you tell me where the away fans sit?

      B Sorry, the *away fans*?

      A Yes, the fans of the visiting team.

D ▶ PAIR WORK **Student A: Go to page 157. Student B: Go to page 159. Follow the instructions.**

3 PRONUNCIATION: Saying /oʊ/ and /ɔ/ vowel sounds

A 🔊 **1.30** Listen to the words. Practice saying them. Do you make the /oʊ/ and /ɔ/ sounds?

   /oʊ/ kn**ow**   /ɔ/ st**ore**

B 🔊 **1.31** Listen and write the words you hear. Which words have the /oʊ/ sound? Which ones have the /ɔ/ sound?

C **Work with a partner. Practice the conversations.**

   A Is this the door to the sports hall?   **B** I'm not sure. I think it's the door to the courts.

   A Can you show me the photos of your store.   **B** Sure. Here are four photos. Do you want more?

4 SPEAKING

A PAIR WORK **Put the conversation in order. Then practice it.**

   ☐ There's a machine outside the class. It sells water.

   [1] Excuse me. I'm looking for the fitness class.

   ☐ Sure. It's on the second floor. Take the stairs – the elevator's out of order.

   ☐ Sorry? Out of order?

   ☐ It finishes at 9:00, I think.

   ☐ 9:00? Great. Just one more thing. Do you know where I can get some water?

   ☐ Yes, it doesn't work. You need to take the stairs.

   ☐ Thank you!

   ☐ Ah! OK, out of order. Got it. Also, could you tell me what time the class finishes?

SWIMMING POOL 🏊

Tues–Fri	10 a.m.–1 p.m.
	3 p.m.–9 p.m.
Sat–Sun	11 a.m.–4 p.m.
Mon	Closed

ENTRANCE – $5.50

B PAIR WORK **Have a conversation with your partner using information about the swimming pool.**

BIKE SHARING

1 LISTENING

FIND IT

A What is bike sharing? Is there a bike-sharing program in your city? You can go online to find out more about it. Would you like to ride a bike in a foreign city? Why or why not?

B Read the introduction to a podcast. Where is Jon? What is he doing?

BICYCLE TRAVELER

New York, Paris, Rio — just three of the many big cities with a popular bike-sharing program. It's clear why these programs are popular: bike riding is a healthy, cheap, and fast way to travel in the city. But what is it like for a visitor? Our reporter Jon Davies spends a day in Mexico City and tries out the *EcoBici* program.

C 🔊 **1.32** **PREDICT** Before his bike ride, does Jon think it's a good idea? Do you think he feels the same after his ride? Listen and check.

D 🔊 **1.32** **LISTEN FOR DETAIL** Listen again and answer the questions.

1 Who usually uses the EcoBici program?
2 How does Marcello use the program?
3 What sometimes happens when cars turn right?
4 What is one problem with the program?
5 What does Marcello do when that happens?
6 How does Jon feel at the end of his ride?

E **PAIR WORK** **THINK CRITICALLY** What are some positive and negative things about bike-sharing programs? Discuss with a partner. Do you think these programs are a good idea for every city? Why or why not?

> I think bike-sharing programs are good because you can get around town fast.

> I don't think they're a good idea because sometimes there are no bikes at the docking stations.

2 PRONUNCIATION: Listening for linking sounds

A 🔊 **1.33** Listen to what Jon says. Focus on the words that link together when Jon says them. Practice saying the sentence slowly. Then say it more quickly. How quickly can you say it?

Cycling‿in Mexico City‿is‿a great way to get around.

B 🔊 **1.34** Draw lines between the linking sounds. Listen and check.

1 How are you feeling?   2 I'll watch out for that.   3 This is basically an enormous traffic jam.

C Complete the rule.

Consonant sounds at the *start / end* of a word usually connect to *consonant / vowel* sounds at the start of the next word.

3 WRITING

A Read the messages. Where do you see messages like this? Which messages are positive, and which are negative?

Tweets   Tweets & replies   Media

 @citizenbrian I'm looking for a station near the pool, but I can NEVER find one, @citibikeride. 0 ⇄ 1 😀

 @davidbarts2 Hey @citibikeride, one of the bikes is broken and no power at the docking station. What do I do? 3 ⇄ 2 😐

 @thelittleone Hi @citibikeride, just to say THANK YOU for putting bikes outside my house. Now I can ride to school, yay! #ridinginthecity 1 ⇄ 11 😎

 @lulu Hi @citibikeride. No bikes at the station near the gym. We need more bikes there, please. 8 ⇄ 0 😋

 @lordaudifan Big bike station on my street, so no space for cars. Now I can't park. :-(Thanks a lot, @citibikeride. 1 ⇄ 2 😕

> **REGISTER** CHECK
>
> In a text message or tweet, you can leave out words:
> *No bikes at the station.*
> When you write the same message as an email, use all the words.
> *There are no bikes at the station.*

B  Look for the words *and*, *but*, and *so* in the messages above. Then complete the sentences.

1 We use _____ to describe the result of an action.

2 We use _____ to add another item to a list of things.

3 We use _____ to present a different choice.

C Match the two parts of the sentences.

1 There are no bikes at the docking station, so

2 It's 45 minutes to work by bus, but

3 When I ride a bike, I exercise and

a by bike it's 20 minutes.

b I get there faster.

c I'm walking to the subway.

WRITE IT

D Use two of your positive points and one of your negative points from exercise 1E on page 28 and write your own messages to the bike-sharing program. Don't forget to use *and*, *but*, and *so*.

TIME TO SPEAK
Fitness programs

FIND IT

A   **RESEARCH**   Look at the sports and fitness activities on the phone. Where are the people, and what are they doing? Read the information on the screen. Go online to find information about free sports and fitness activities where you live, if you can.

B   **DISCUSS**   What are the positive things about free fitness programs? What other types of free activities are usually available in a town? In a school? Use the phrases at the bottom of the page to help you.

C   **PREPARE**   Design a fitness program for your town, workplace, or school. Use your ideas from A and B. Think about …

- **activities** Choose four different activities.
- **location(s)** You can choose one place or a few.
- **timetable** When do people do these activities? How often do they do them?
- **people** Who is it for, and why?

D   **PRESENT**   Tell the class about your fitness program. Listen to the suggestions from the other groups. Which ideas do you like? Why?

E   **AGREE**   Your town can have two new fitness programs. Discuss which two programs to choose. Make a decision as a class.

YOUNG OR OLD, we have an activity for you!

Find out today what **FREE** fitness programs there are in your city!

To check your progress, go to page 153.

USEFUL PHRASES

DISCUSS
Free fitness programs are good because …
Free fitness programs help people to …
What do you think?

PREPARE
What about (soccer/swimming/tennis, etc.)?
Where can people do them?
What time is good for people/parents/students?
How does it help?

PRESENT
Our program is called …
It helps people because …
Any questions?

REVIEW 1 (UNITS 1–3)

1 VOCABULARY

A **Read the words. Which word doesn't belong in each category? Circle it.**

1 People you know: grandson   coworker   girlfriend   (player)   classmate   6
2 Everyday things: boss   keychain   candy bar   hand lotion   umbrella   ___
3 Expressions with *have*: a snack   free time   something to drink   the laundry   a party   ___
4 Expressions with *do*: some work   the laundry   housework   some coffee   the dishes   ___
5 Work and study: calendar   textbook   document   push   Wi-Fi   ___
6 Sports words: court   pool   team   screen   race   ___
7 Exercising: stretch   cash   throw   jump   turn   ___

B **Look at the words you circled in exercise 1A. Where do those words really belong? Write the category number (1–7).**

C **Add three more words or phrases that you know to each category.**

2 GRAMMAR

A **Circle the correct words to complete the conversations.**

1 **A** What do you have in ¹*your / her* bag?
  B ²*The / My* sunglasses and ³*my wife's umbrella / the umbrella of my wife*.
  A Why? It ⁴*doesn't rain / isn't raining* right now.
  B No, it ⁵*isn't / aren't*, but ⁶*often it / it often* rains here in the fall.

2 **A** Who are ⁷*that / these* people in the picture?
  B Max and Sacha.
  A I ⁸*doesn't / don't* know them. ⁹*Do / Does* they work with you?
  B No, they ¹⁰*isn't / aren't* my coworkers. They're my neighbors. They ¹¹*lives / live* next door.
  A I see. And ¹²*who / whose* head is that in the photo?
  B Ha! It's mine!

B PAIR WORK **Practice reading the conversations.**

3 SPEAKING

PAIR WORK **Describe your routine to your partner. Ask and answer the questions.**

■ What do you usually do during the week? And on the weekend?
■ What are you doing today? Are you doing anything that is different from normal?

> I usually work during the week. On weekends, I exercise or go to the gym. I love sports.

> These days, I'm learning to play hockey. It's great!

4 FUNCTIONAL LANGUAGE

A **Circle the correct options to complete the conversation.**

A Hi, Carol. Long time no see!

B Hi, Leo. ¹*Nice to see you again! / nice to meet you!*

A How are you?

B I'm good. This is a great ²*place / weather*, isn't it? The house is beautiful.

A Yeah, really great. It's my first time here. Do you know ³*anybody / some person* here?

B I know everyone! It's my close friend's party.

A So, you know Max? ⁴*Actually? / Seriously?* Wow! I know him from school.
So, you know the house, too, right?

B Yeah.

A Good. Can you ⁵*know / tell me* where the kitchen is? I'm really hungry.

B Me, too! Come on, it's this way.

B **Two friends are having problems with their connection. Complete their conversation with the verbs in the box.**

call	catch	hear	is	say	try

A Hi, can you ¹_____ me OK?

B No, the connection is terrible.

A OK, let me ²_____ you. OK?

B Sorry, can you ³_____ that again? I didn't ⁴_____ that.

A I said, "Let me call you."

B OK, I'm sorry, it's my Wi-Fi.

A How about now? ⁵_____ that any better?

B No, sorry. Let's ⁶_____ again later.

5 SPEAKING

A PAIR WORK **Choose one of the situations. Act it out in pairs.**

1 You are at a party. Talk to somebody you don't know. Talk about the people at the party, the place, the weather, etc. Think of some surprising information to tell your partner.

   A Hello, I'm [name].

   B Hi, [name]. I'm [name]. Nice to meet you.

2 You are talking to a friend online. There is a problem with the internet connection. Explain the problem. Ask for repetition to check the problem. Decide what you are going to do to solve it.

   A Hi, how are you doing? It's so nice to speak to you again.

   B Hi! How are you? Listen, I can't hear you very well …

3 You are in a large sports store. You want to buy a souvenir of your favorite team. Ask the sales clerk for information about where to find things. Check the information before you finish the conversation.

   A Excuse me, can you help us? We're looking for …

   B Sure, all the souvenirs are …

B **Change roles and repeat the role play.**

UNIT OBJECTIVES
- talk about your plans
- talk about giving and receiving gifts
- make and respond to invitations
- write an online event announcement
- choose gifts for your host

GOOD TIMES

4

START SPEAKING

A **Look at the picture. What is happening? Do you think they're having a good time? Do you have similar events in your country?**

B **Which things are important for special events (for example, a cake for a birthday party)? Why? Can you think of other things connected to special occasions?**

cake	dancing	family
fireworks	food	friends
games	gifts	music

REAL STUDENT

Is your family celebration the same as Irene's?

C **What special days do you have with your family? What do you usually do? For ideas, watch Irene's video.**

1 VOCABULARY: Describing pop culture

FIND IT

A 🔊 **1.35** **What do you know about Comic Con? Look at the pictures. Which things can you find at Comic Con? You can go online to find out more. Listen and repeat the words.**

actor

director

DIRECTOR

a **TV show**

fans playing **video games**

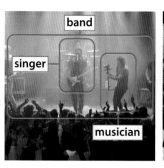

band

singer

musician

a **concert**

artist

an arts **festival**

B **PAIR WORK** **With your partner, think of examples of these things.**

one famous artist   *two* popular video games   *three* TV shows
three movie actors   *four* bands / singers / musicians   *two* movie directors

C ▶ **Now do the vocabulary exercises for 4.1 on page 143.**

2 LANGUAGE IN CONTEXT

A **Read Cassie's blog post. Which words from exercise 1A does she use in her post?**

Fangirl 😎 **Superhero**

Blog   About

So excited! Comic Con is coming here this weekend. Yay! Tommy and I have our new costumes, and they look totally cool!

Here's my Comic Con Top 3.

1. Movies! Don't miss the Star Trek celebration on Saturday. You can meet some of the actors and directors from the TV shows and movies. Can't wait! 😊 I'm bringing my camera, so check out next week's post for photos.

2. Games! The gaming hall is 2,000m² of games, games, and more games!

3. Art! Guess what? Tommy is showing his pictures at Artists' Alley this year. 😊 He isn't selling anything, but you can order from his website.

Are you going to Comic Con? What are you doing?
Add a comment and tell me about it.

GLOSSARY
fangirl (*n*) a female fan who loves comics, films, and/or music
costume (*n*) clothes you wear to look like someone else

B **Read the blog again. Check (✓) the sentence(s) that are true. Correct the false ones.**

☐ 1 Cassie doesn't like her costume.

☐ 2 You can meet famous people from TV and movies.

☐ 3 Tommy wants to sell his pictures at Comic Con.

3 GRAMMAR: Present continuous for future plans

A **Circle the correct options to complete the rules. Use the sentences in the grammar box to help you.**

1 You **can / can't** use the present continuous for the future.

2 Use the present continuous for **plans or arrangements / predictions**.

> **Present continuous for future plans**
>
> Comic Con **is coming** this weekend.   I'm bringing my camera.   **Are** you **going** to Comic Con?

B ▶ **Now go to page 132. Look at the grammar chart and do the grammar exercise for 4.1.**

C 🔊 **1.36** **Complete the sentences with the present continuous form of the verb in parentheses ( ). Listen and check. Then read the conversation in pairs.**

INSIDER ENGLISH

Say *No way!* when you're really surprised to hear something.

A What ¹ ___are___ you ___doing___ (do) on Saturday?

B We ² _____ (go) to the music festival in the afternoon.

A Yeah? I ³ _____ (go), too! My brother's band ⁴ _____ (play).

B No way! When ⁵ _____ he _____ (play)?

A At 8:30, on the new music stage.

B Oh, no! We ⁶ _____ (not stay) that long.

D PAIR WORK **Look at the activities. Ask and answer questions about this weekend with your partner.**

> go to a concert   go to the movies   see friends   study   visit family   work

> *Are you going to the movies this weekend?*   *Yeah. We're seeing the new Star Wars movie.*

4 SPEAKING

GROUP WORK **What is your group doing between this class and the next one? Find a time when you can all meet.**

> *What are you doing after class, Ricardo?*   *I'm meeting my sister for dinner.*

> *Are you doing anything tomorrow?*   *Tomorrow? No, I'm free all day.*

1 VOCABULARY: Naming gift items

Gift ideas for **him or her**

1. a bouquet of flowers
2. a candle
3. some candy
4. a gift card
5. some jewelry
6. some perfume
7. a phone charger
8. a purse
9. some speakers
10. a sweatshirt

A 1.37 **Are you a difficult person to buy gifts for? Why? Look at the gifts. Listen and say the words. Which gifts would you like?**

B PAIR WORK **Imagine you are buying gifts for friends and family. Who would like each of these gifts?**

C ▶ **Now do the vocabulary exercises for 4.2 on page 144.**

2 LANGUAGE IN CONTEXT

A 1.38 **Listen to three people talking about gifts. Which gifts from exercise 1A does each person say?**

B 1.38 **Listen again and read. Why are these people difficult to buy gifts for?**

Lara's dad   Rosa and her brothers   Hasan's sister

Lara

Hasan

Rosa

◀) **1.38 Audio script**

Lara It's really difficult to find a gift for my dad. He always tells me he doesn't want anything. In the end, I usually get him something boring like a **sweatshirt** or socks. This year I'm going for something a little different. I'm buying him an experience – a **gift card**, for one hour of driving a really fast sports car. I hope he likes it. It wasn't cheap!

Hasan My little sister's very difficult. I never know what gift to get her. I sometimes buy **perfume** or clothes for her, but she never likes them. Or I take her to a movie, but she doesn't want to watch it. This year I'm giving her a **bouquet of flowers**. Who doesn't like flowers?

Rosa Mom and dad never know what gifts to get for me and my brothers. They usually buy us books or a watch. This year we're asking them for gift cards. Then we can get what we really want in our favorite stores.

C ◀) 1.39 **Are the people happy when they get their gifts? Listen and check.**

3 GRAMMAR: Object pronouns

A Read the sentences in the grammar box. Then find the people and things in the text on page 36 that the words in bold replace.

> **Object pronouns**
>
> He always tells **me** he doesn't want anything. I never know what gift to get **her**.
>
> I usually get **him** something boring. I buy perfume or clothes, but she never likes **them**.
>
> I hope he likes **it**. I take her to a movie, but she doesn't want to watch **it**.
>
> Mom and dad never know what gifts to get for **me** and my brothers.
>
> They usually buy **us** books or a watch.
>
> This year we're asking **them** for gift cards.

B Which object pronouns in the grammar box refer to:

a people? _____ _____ _____ _____ _____

b objects? _____ _____

c both? _____

C ▶ Now go to page 133. Look at the grammar chart and do the grammar exercise for 4.2.

D Replace the words in parentheses with object pronouns. Then check your accuracy. Tell your partner about the things you buy for the people in your family.

1 My dad loves cooking. I always buy cookbooks for (my dad) _____him_____ . He loves (cookbooks) _____ .

2 My sister is difficult to buy for. I usually get (my sister) _____ gift cards to her favorite stores. She likes (gift cards) _____ because she can choose the clothes she wants.

3 Music is my parents' passion. They love (music) _____ ! It's really easy to buy a gift for (my parents) _____ .

> ✓ **ACCURACY** CHECK
>
> Use *it* or *them* after *like.*
>
> Thank you, it's beautiful. I really ~~like~~! ✗
> Thank you, it's beautiful. I really like it! ✓

4 SPEAKING

PAIR WORK Imagine you want to buy some gifts. Choose three people you know and decide what to get for them. For ideas, watch Caio's video.

- a neighbor – he/she often helps you
- your boss – it's his/her last day at work
- a teenager – he/she loves technology
- a young child – it's his/her birthday
- a close friend – he/she is feeling sad
- your teacher – a thank-you gift

I want to get something for my art teacher for her birthday.

How about a bouquet of flowers? She can paint a picture of them.

REAL STUDENT

Do you want to buy the same things as Caio?

4.3 I'D LOVE TO!

1 FUNCTIONAL LANGUAGE

A ◀)) **1.40** **Read and listen to the phone calls and voicemails. Where do the friends plan to meet? Where do they meet in the end?**

◀)) **1.40 Audio script**

A Hey Mika, are you doing anything later? We're going to that street festival downtown. **Would you like to** come?

B Oh, **sorry**, Daniel, **I can't. I wish I could, but** I'm working on my paper today.

A Come on! You can work on your paper later.

B That's true. OK. **I'd love to.**

A Great! **We can meet you** at three at the subway station.

B **See you there!**

(3:00 p.m.)

B Hi! I'm at the subway station. Where are you?

(3:05 p.m.)

A Sorry, Mika. Just got your message. We're running late. **Let's meet** at that new pizza place on Third Street. **See you soon.**

(3:15 p.m.)

B Hey, Daniel. It's me again. I'm outside the restaurant now. Are you guys close?

A We're here now. Where are you? Oh, wait, I can see you!

!	*a guy* = a man	*guys* = a group of people, any number, men and/or women
	That guy over there lives in my building.	*I'll meet you guys at the elevator in five minutes.* *Hey, guys! What's up?*

B **Complete the chart with expressions in bold from the conversation and voicemails above.**

Invite someone	Would you ¹_____ to (come)?
Accept	I'd ²_____ to!
Don't accept	Sorry, Daniel, I ³_____ .
	I ⁴_____ I could, but (I'm working on my paper).
Suggest when and where to meet	We ⁵_____ meet you (at a quarter after / at the subway).
	Let's ⁶_____ (at the pizza place / later).
Agree on a plan	⁷_____ you there!
	See you ⁸_____ .

C **PAIR WORK** **Practice the conversations and voicemails in exercise 1A with your partner.**

2 REAL-WORLD STRATEGY

A 🔊 **1.41** **Listen to Lucca and Jen. Where does Lucca want to go? Does Jen want to go?**

MAKING GENERAL EXCUSES

When you don't want to accept an invitation because you have a lot to do, give a general reason followed by the suggestion of much more.

*I don't know. I have homework **and stuff**.*

*I'm not sure. I have family visiting **and things**.*

*Maybe, but I'm getting ready to go on vacation **and everything**.*

B 🔊 **1.41** **Read the information in the box above. Then listen again and complete Lucca and Jen's conversation with words from the box.**

Lucca Hi, Jen. What's up?

Jen Not much.

Lucca Are you doing anything later?
We're going to the concert in the park.

Jen ¹ _____ .

I have work and then the gym
² _____ .

Lucca Come on! It'll be fun.

Jen ³ _____ next time.

C ⬚ PAIR WORK ⬚ **Imagine someone invites you to these events. Refuse the invitation and give a general excuse. Practice with your partner.**

- a music festival in the park on Saturday and Sunday
- a video game competition all day tomorrow, two hours from where you live
- a band at a local café tonight, 9:00 p.m. to midnight

3 PRONUNCIATION: Saying /v/ in the middle of a word

A 🔊 **1.42** **Listen to the words. Focus on the /v/ sound. Practice saying the sound.**

1 lo**v**e   2 ha**v**e   3 e**v**erything   4 festi**v**al

B 🔊 **1.43** **Listen. Who pronounces the /v/ sound? Circle A or B.**

1 **A** Would you like to come to the street festi**v**al?

   B I'd lo**v**e to.

2 **A** Hi **Viv**ian! Do you want to go to the concert with us?

   B Sorry, I can't. I ha**v**e work and e**v**erything.

3 **A** We're going to a **v**ideo game competition. Would you like to come?

   B Sorry, I can't. I'm going to a music festi**v**al.

C **Practice the conversations in exercise 3B with a partner.**

4 SPEAKING

FIND IT

⬚ PAIR WORK ⬚ **Student A: Think of an event that is happening in your town or city. You can also use your phone to find an event.**
Then invite your partner.
Student B: Say no at first.
Then change your mind.

4.4 WAITING FOR SOMETHING SPECIAL

1 LISTENING

Congress Avenue Bridge Austin, Texas

rock concert

bats

Batman

A **PREDICT** Look at the pictures from an unusual event. Can you guess what it is?

B ◄)) **1.44** Listen to a news report about the event. Was your prediction correct?

C ◄)) **1.44** **LISTEN FOR DETAIL** Listen to the report again and answer the questions.

1 Where does the festival take place?

2 Where do the bats come from?

3 What moment are the people waiting for?

4 How many bats are there?

D ◄)) **1.45** **PAIR WORK** What other things do you think happen at the festival? Think of four to six possibilities. Listen and check your ideas.

E **THINK CRITICALLY** Not everyone in Austin likes the festival. Think of who these people are. Why don't they enjoy it? Would you like to go to the festival? Why or why not?

2 PRONUNCIATION: Listening for single sounds

A ◄)) **1.46** Listen. Focus on the letters in **bold**. Can you hear one or two sounds?

1 We know them from ba**d d**reams.

2 Bats a**r**e **r**eally scary.

3 There**'s s**o much happening.

B ◄)) **1.47** Find two letters in the sentences that can connect to make one sound. There are two pairs of letters in sentence 1. Listen and check.

1 They can eat ten thousand kilograms of insects in one night.

2 It's home to music festivals and car racing.

3 I can't wait to try the barbecue.

C **Complete the sentence.**

Two sounds often become *one / three* if they are *similar / different* at the end of a word and the start of the next word.

3 WRITING

A Read the online event announcement for another unusual festival. Would you like to go to Bug Fest? Why or why not?

BugFest

September 19, 1:00 p.m.
City Museum of Science

Welcome to Bug Fest!
A celebration of the wonderful world of insects! Come and join us on the 19th and find out why we love bugs. There's something for everyone!

> *All day*
  Scientists from the museum are presenting their favorite bugs.
> *12:00–3:00 p.m.*
  Our team of top chefs is also cooking some great insect dishes.
> *10:00 a.m.–1:00 p.m.*
  Two local artists are painting the bugs. You can paint them, too.
> *1:00 p.m.–late*
  We have music as well! Local bands are playing in the museum gardens.

B **WRITING SKILLS** Find the words *also*, *as well*, and *too* in the announcement. What do they all mean?

  a in addition   b to finish

C Look at the announcement again. Check (✓) the information you can see.

  activities ☐   address ☐   date ☐   place ☐   price ☐   time ☐

WRITE IT

D Write an event announcement. Follow the instructions in the form.

  Add the name of your event here.

  Add the time and/or date here.

  Add the location here.

  Add a short description here (max 30 words).

E **GROUP WORK** Look at your group's event announcements. Write a short comment on each one saying that you will go or explaining why you can't. If you decide to go, say what interests you about each event.

TIME TO SPEAK
The gift of giving

A **Think about these questions:**

■ When you travel to another city or country, what gifts do you bring back for your friends and family?

■ What kinds of things do you like to receive as gifts?

■ Look at the gift ideas on the right. Are they good to choose for your family and friends?

■ What other gifts do you prefer to give them?

B **DISCUSS** Imagine you are going to stay with a friend in another country next week. You are going to give your host two gifts: (a) something typical from your town or region and (b) something funny. You can only spend $50. Consider the following things.

■ How are you traveling? (Plane? Train?)

■ Is your host male or female?

■ Is your host old or young?

C **PRESENT** Tell the class about your gifts. Explain why you made these choices and how much you're going to spend.

D **AGREE** Which gifts are (a) unusual or interesting, and (b) very typical of your region? Choose the two gifts to give your host.

To check your progress, go to page 154.

USEFUL PHRASES

DISCUSS
What do you think of … ?
What's a typical gift from our town?
I love this gift because …

PRESENT
We're buying … because …
We're spending $20 on …

AGREE
I think so, too.
Good idea.
I like that idea a lot.

- talk about past events in your life
- ask questions about the past
- congratulate and sympathize with people
- write a comment agreeing or disagreeing with an online post
- summarize a story

FIRSTS AND LASTS

5

START SPEAKING

A **Look at the picture. Where are the children? What are they doing for the first time? Are they all happy? Why or why not?**

B **Think of a special picture of you as a child. What are you doing in the picture? Where are you? Is anyone else there? For ideas, watch Allison's video.**

REAL STUDENT

Is your picture different from Allison's?

ONE AMAZING DAY

1 LANGUAGE IN CONTEXT

A **Look at the photos below. What are the people doing for the first time? Are their experiences positive or negative? Why do you think so? Read their stories. Were your answers correct?**

A day to remember.

I live in Colorado, in the middle of the USA. For my 45th birthday, I visited the ocean for the first time in my life. It was amazing. My friends weren't with me, but I stayed on the beach for hours. It was the perfect birthday.

Carol

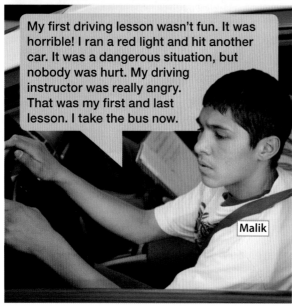

My first driving lesson wasn't fun. It was horrible! I ran a red light and hit another car. It was a dangerous situation, but nobody was hurt. My driving instructor was really angry. That was my first and last lesson. I take the bus now.

Malik

Barbara

My most amazing day was when I went to Rio to run in the marathon. It was my first visit to Rio, and it was my first marathon. My time was 4:57! I was so tired when I crossed the finish line. It was a very proud moment.

GLOSSARY

run a red light (v) drive through a red traffic light
marathon (n) a running race of 26 miles (42 kilometers)

B **Complete the sentences with the names *Carol*, *Malik*, or *Barbara*. Whose story do you find most interesting? Why?**

1 _____ describes an accident.

2 _____ talks about a competition.

3 _____ talks about a birthday.

4 _____ says where he/she lives.

2 VOCABULARY: Describing opinions and feelings

A 🔊 **1.48** **Match the four adjectives in the box with the correct emojis below. Then find and <u>underline</u> eight more adjectives in the stories on page 44. Match them with the other emojis. Listen and check.**

~~cool~~	crazy	loud	strange

1 _____cool_____ P   5 _____   9 _____

2 _____   6 _____   10 _____

3 _____   7 _____   11 _____

4 _____   8 _____   12 _____

B **Decide if each adjective is generally positive (*P*), negative (*N*), or can be both (*B*).**

C ▶ **Now do the vocabulary exercises for 5.1 on page 145.**

D PAIR WORK **Look at the words in the box. Use the words from exercise 2A to describe them.**

bike-sharing programs	birthdays	concerts	fast cars
festivals	my street	soccer	video games

> Bike sharing programs are fun.

> I don't know. I think biking in the city is dangerous.

3 GRAMMAR: Simple past

A **Complete the rules below. Use the sentences in the grammar box to help you.**

1 The simple past of *be* is _____ or *were*. The negative is *wasn't* or _____.

2 The simple past of regular verbs ends in *-ed*. For example, _____.

3 The simple past of irregular verbs doesn't end in *-ed*. For example, _____.

Simple past

I **visited** the ocean for the first time in my life.   It **was** my first marathon.

I **ran** a red light and **hit** another car.   My friends **weren't** with me.

B ▶ **Now go to page 133. Look at the grammar chart and do the grammar exercise for 5.1.**

C **Marina is talking about her first love. Complete the text with the simple past of the verbs in the box.**

be	go	live	move	not be	talk

I remember my first love very well. His name ¹_____ Raúl. We ²_____ on the same street, and we ³_____ to the same school. He was funny, and he always ⁴_____ about cool and interesting things. We ⁵_____ together for a long time because his family ⁶_____ to another city, but I have very nice memories of him.

D PAIR WORK **Think about an important person in your life when you were younger. Tell your partner about this person. Use the simple past.**

4 SPEAKING

PAIR WORK **Think of a special day in your life. Where were you? Who was with you? What happened? Was it a good or a bad experience? Tell your partner.**

5.2 GUESS IN 60 SECONDS

1 VOCABULARY: Describing life events

A 🔊 **1.49** **Listen and say the life events. Write five of them under the pictures.**

be born	buy a house or apartment	graduate from college	get married
get a job	become a grandparent	have a baby	retire (stop working)
buy a car	meet your future wife/husband	learn to drive	start school

A _____ B _____ C _____ D _____ E _____

B **PAIR WORK** **Write the 12 life events in the order that they usually happen. Compare with a partner. Are they in the same order? Explain your choices.**

C ▶ **Now do the vocabulary exercises for 5.2 on page 145.**

2 LANGUAGE IN CONTEXT

A 🔊 **1.50** **Look at the pictures. Can you guess the famous man? Listen to Carla try to guess. Number the pictures in the order you hear them.**

🔊 **1.50 Audio script**

Carla **Was** he **born** in 1954?

Host Yes, he was.

Carla And did he die in 1989?

Host No, he didn't. He died in 2011.

Carla Hmm, when did he retire?

Host He **retired** in 1989.

Carla OK! Umm. Did he study medicine?

Host Yes, he did.

Carla OK. The "six." That's difficult. I don't know. Did he **get married** six times?

Host No, he didn't.

Carla Did he **buy** six **cars**?

Host No, he didn't. Think about family …

Carla Children! How many children did he have?

Host He had six children. Correct! You have ten seconds.

Carla Did he come from Argentina?

Host No, he didn't come from Argentina.

Carla Did he come from Brazil?

Host Yes, he did!

Carla OK. Sports. Was he an athlete?

Host Yes, but what was the sport? And we're out of time. Carla, for $1,000, who is the famous person?

B   **Write six sentences about the famous person in exercise 2A.**
    He was born in 1954.

C   🔊 **1.51** **Who is the famous person? Listen and check. Were you right?**

3   GRAMMAR: Simple past negative and questions

A   **Complete the rules. Use the sentences in the grammar box to help you.**
    1   Use _____ when you ask a question.
    2   Use _____ to make a negative.
    3   The main verb in questions and negatives **is / isn't** in the simple past.

Simple past negative and questions	
Did he **die** in 1989?	No, he **didn't**. He died in 2011.
Did he **come** from Argentina?	He **didn't come** from Argentina.

B   🔊 **1.52** **Look at these verbs from exercise 1A on page 46. Write the correct simple past form. Listen and say the words.**
    1   get _____   3   become _____   5   meet _____
    2   have _____   4   buy _____

C   ▶ **Now go to page 134. Look at the grammar chart and do the grammar exercise for 5.2.**

D   PAIR WORK **Correct these false statements about the famous person using the simple past negative. Then check your accuracy.**
    1   He had seven children.
    2   He studied French.
    3   He came from Mexico.
    4   He became a soccer player in 1954.
    5   He died in 1989.

    He didn't have seven children. He had six children.

    ✔ **ACCURACY** CHECK
    Don't use the simple past after *did* or *didn't* in questions and negatives.
    I didn't ~~studied~~ last night. ✗
    I didn't study last night. ✓

4   SPEAKING

PAIR WORK **Draw six small pictures about what you did last weekend. Ask your partner questions about their pictures. Ask for extra information. For ideas, watch Irene's video.**

Did you go for coffee last weekend?
Yes, I did.
Where did you go?

REAL STUDENT
Did you do the same things last weekend as Irene?

THAT'S COOL!

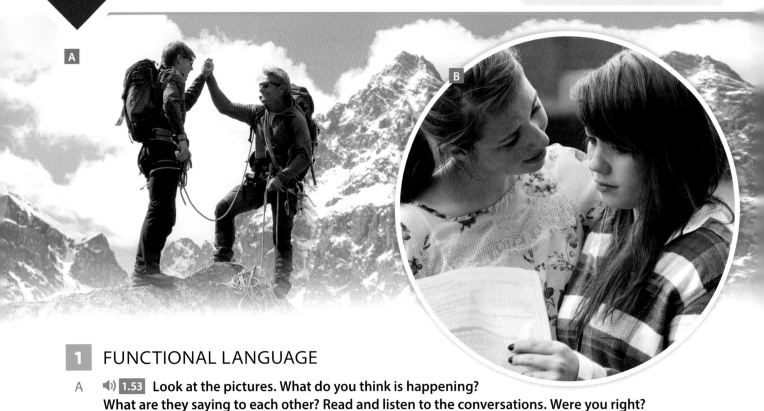

1 FUNCTIONAL LANGUAGE

A 🔊 **1.53** **Look at the pictures. What do you think is happening? What are they saying to each other? Read and listen to the conversations. Were you right?**

🔊 1.53 Audio script

1 **A** Hey, I made it!! What a fantastic experience!

B **Congratulations**, Johnny! **Great job**!

A It was really scary at the top!

B You're right, it wasn't easy, and the weather was terrible.

A Not bad for my first time, huh?

B **You did really well.** I'm proud of you.

A You know what? Now, I want to climb another mountain.

B **That's great news**! Let's do it!

2 **A** Oh, no! I failed my chemistry final.

B **I'm so sorry**, Ana.

A I failed by two points!

B **That's terrible! Talk about bad luck.**

A I know, right? Oh, I can't believe this!

B **Never mind.** You can take the class again over the summer.

A Really?

B Yes, **don't worry about it**, Ana. **It's not the end of the world.**

B **Complete the chart with expressions in bold from the conversations above.**

Congratulations (good news)	Sympathy (bad news)
Congratulations!	I'm so ⁴_____.
¹_____ job!	That's terrible! Talk about ⁵_____.
You did ²_____ !	⁶_____ mind.
That's ³_____ news!	Don't worry about it. It's not ⁷_____.

C **PAIR WORK** **Practice the conversations in exercise 1A with a partner. Then change the good and bad news and practice again.**

2 REAL-WORLD STRATEGY

A 🔊 **1.54 Listen to a short conversation. What test did the person take? What information does the person get wrong?**

> **CHECKING YOUR UNDERSTANDING**
>
> When you want to check your understanding of what someone said, you can ask a question with *mean*.
>
> *You mean … ?*   *So, you mean … .*
> *Do you mean … ?*   *I thought you said … .*
>
> The reply often includes the phrase, *I meant … .*

B 🔊 **1.55 Read the information in the box above about checking your understanding. Then complete another short conversation with one of the questions from the box. Listen and check.**

A Well, I failed my driver's test.

B Oh, I'm so sorry.

A Why? It's amazing! I can finally drive!

B But _____ you *failed* the test?

A No! Ha! I meant "passed," not "failed." Duh! I passed my driver's test. I'm just so excited!!

C ▶ PAIR WORK **Student A go to page 157. Student B go to page 159. Follow the instructions.**

3 PRONUNCIATION: Saying the stress in words

A 🔊 **1.56 Listen to the words. How many syllables do you hear in each word?**

1 amazing 3	3 congratulations ___	5 impressed ___
2 sorry ___	4 terrible ___	6 fantastic ___

B 🔊 **1.57 Listen. Which speaker, A or B, uses word stress clearly?**

	A B		A B		A B
1 amazing	☐ ☐	3 fantastic	☐ ☐	5 terrible	☐ ☐
2 congratulations	☐ ☐	4 horrible	☐ ☐		

C GROUP WORK **Practice the conversations below. Take turns being A, B, and C. Focus on word stress.**

1 **A** I passed my driving test.
   B That's amazing!
   C You did really well.

2 **A** I got the job!
   B Congratulations!
   C That's fantastic!

3 **A** How was the test?
   B I failed. It was horrible!
   C Yes, it was terrible! I failed, too.

4 SPEAKING

PAIR WORK **Read the situations. Practice responding to the news with your partner.**

1 Your old friend tells you that he or she got married recently. Congratulate him/her on the news.

2 A coworker of yours didn't get the job he/she really wanted. Sympathize and try to make him/her feel better.

3 Your neighbors' daughter just found out that she is going to a very good university. Congratulate her.

4 Your favorite teacher was in a car accident. He isn't hurt, but his car is totally dead. He loved that car. Sympathize with him.

1 READING

A **PAIR WORK** Look at the pictures. Which picture is Chicago? Which is Bristol? Which is Melbourne?

B **READ FOR MAIN IDEAS** Read the posts. What kind of website is this? Who is positive, and who is negative about their first day?

A stranger in a strange town

Rafael: I went to Chicago about ten years ago for a work project. I remember the moment I stepped off the bus from the airport. Everything was strange – the smells, the crowds, the language – and everyone was in a hurry. The weather was also very cold. I needed warm clothes, and fast! In Mexico, we don't have winters like that!

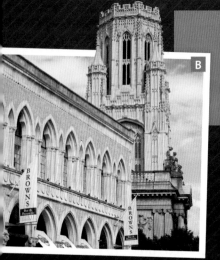

Julia: I'm from Cologne in Germany. At age 20 I went to the U.K. as an exchange student. I remember my first day at the university in Bristol. It was scary, but then I looked around and saw so many other people in my situation. I thought, "They must feel the same." That helped. And it was a beautiful September day. Suddenly, I felt so positive.

Kamal: I was born in Nepal, but I went to live in Melbourne, Australia, as an immigrant worker. On that first day, I didn't understand any English, but I remember that people were friendly. I smiled, and they smiled back. I walked along the river and felt very free. Everything was clean and new, like a fresh start.

✉ Send your first impressions to 1stday@ourplanet.com

C **READ FOR DETAILS** Read the posts again. Check (✓) the sentences that are true. Correct the false ones.
- [ ] 1 Rafael was prepared for his arrival in Chicago.
- [ ] 2 The weather is different in Rafael's country.
- [ ] 3 Julia went to Bristol for work.
- [ ] 4 Julia felt very scared and alone, and those feelings never changed.
- [ ] 5 When he arrived, Kamal already knew some English.
- [ ] 6 For Kamal, his first day was like a new beginning.

D **PAIR WORK** **THINK CRITICALLY** Imagine what these people say about your hometown. Do they say the same things or different things?
- an exchange student from another country
- a businessperson
- an immigrant worker

WRITING

A   Look at these comments on the posts in exercise 1B. Match them to the correct posts. Write *R* (Rafael),
    J (Julia), or *K* (Kamal).

Tweets   Tweets & replies   Media

1   **@tobytwo: I know the feeling,** I didn't understand a word of English on my first day.
    It was just terrible!

2   **@TheresaB: Interesting, but** my first days in the U.K. weren't like that. It rained
    and rained. ☺

3   **@cigdemyilmaz4: No way!** I didn't like being an exchange student at all. I missed my
    home all the time. Didn't you miss it?

4   **@patricianuñez12: Are you kidding?** So what if the weather isn't the best? It's a great
    town! Buy a coat and keep an open mind.

5   **@daviddaly: Absolutely!** ☺ My first day in San Diego was the same – all those people,
    all those strange sounds and smells – it was amazing, actually!

6   **@titusx2: You're so right.** I hated Canada when I arrived – so cold and unfriendly – but
    I call it home now. Don't trust your first ideas about something!

B   Which of the six comments agree with the posts? Which disagree?

C   **WRITING SKILLS** Look at the expressions in **bold** in the comments. Are they to agree or disagree?

    Agree: *I know the feeling,* _____ , _____

    Disagree: *Interesting, but … ,* _____ , _____

 **WRITE IT**

D   Write a comment to Rafael, Julia, or Kamal agreeing or disagreeing
    with their posts. Use the expressions in exercise 2C. Why do you
    agree or disagree? What information should you include?

REGISTER CHECK

You can say *Are you crazy?,*
Seriously?, Are you kidding?
when the person is a friend
or someone you know well.

HOME IS WHERE THE ♥ IS

TIME TO SPEAK
Iceberg!

The Titanic left Southampton, England, for New York on April 10, 1912. It was the ship's first time at sea.	The Titanic hit an iceberg off the coast of Canada on April 14. It made a hole, and the ship started to sink very quickly.	Some passengers and crew escaped on lifeboats. Survivors were rescued by another ship, the Carpathia, on April 15.

FIND IT

A   **RESEARCH**   Look at the pictures and read the captions. What do you know about the story of the Titanic? If you can, go online to see more pictures and learn the full story of the famous accident.

B   **PREPARE**   You are going to read a story about a person who was on the Titanic. Divide into four groups (A, B, C, and D) and follow the instructions for your group. Then answer the questions below and take notes.

> **Group A: Go to page 157.**
> **Group B: Go to page 158.**

> **Group C: Go to page 159.**
> **Group D: Go to page 160.**

1   How old was the person?
2   Where was the person from?
3   Was the person a passenger or a crew member? If a passenger, what type of ticket did the person have?
4   Did the person survive? If so, how?
5   What did the person do in the years after the accident?

C   **PRESENT**   Make new groups with one person each from groups A, B, C, and D. Tell your new group about your person using your notes. Take notes on the other stories that you hear.

> We read about Carla Jensen. She was from Denmark and was only 19. She traveled …

D   **DISCUSS**   Discuss all the people in your stories. What do they all have in common? How are they different? Whose story do you like most? Why?

> Carla traveled third class. She didn't have much money, but Molly was rich …

To check your progress, go to page 154.

USEFUL PHRASES

RESEARCH
The picture shows …
What does it say about … ?
I can't find the answer. Where does it tell you about … ?

PRESENT
Our group read about …
After that … / Then … / Later …

DISCUSS
They all traveled/survived/worked …
I thought his/her story was really sad/inspiring/interesting.
I liked this story most because …

UNIT OBJECTIVES

- plan a shopping trip
- talk about shopping habits
- describe what you want in a store
- write a script for a vlog
- present an idea for a new invention

BUY NOW, PAY LATER

6

START SPEAKING

A   **Look at the picture. Where are the people? What are they doing?**

B   **How often do you go shopping? What type of things do you usually buy?**

C   **Is there a market like the one in the picture where you live? Do you shop there? What other places do you go shopping? For ideas, watch Irene's video.**

REAL STUDENT

Do you agree with Irene?

53

BLACK FRIDAY FUN

1 LANGUAGE IN CONTEXT

FIND IT

A 🔊 **1.58** PAIR WORK **What do you know about Black Friday? You can go online to find out more. Then listen to four people talking about Black Friday. Who likes the day?**

B 🔊 **1.58** **Listen to the program again. Who … ?**

1 _____ wants a new television.
2 _____ works at the store.

3 _____ is with someone.
4 _____ made a mistake.

🔊 **1.58 Audio script**

Black Friday is back! We asked some people what they think of it. Here's what they said.

Katie I didn't know today was Black Friday. I only came here to **return** a shirt but forget it! I'm going to come back next week – when it's not so crazy!

Seb I love Black Friday. I **save** for months and months and even **borrow** money from friends. I go crazy! I usually **spend** my money on clothes and shoes, but this year I'm going to buy a TV.

Marcia I hate Black Friday! I have to work all day and, excuse me… . Are you going to buy that?

Adam I'm here with my wife, but I can't find her now! I really want to go home. We're not going to come back next year. We're going to **shop online** in the future.

C PAIR WORK **Do you think Black Friday is a good idea? Why or why not?**

2 VOCABULARY: Using money

A 🔊 **1.59** **Listen and say the words. Then match the words to the correct definition.**

borrow ☐	cost ☐	lend ☐	pay back ☐	return ☐
save ☐	sell ☐	shop online 1	spend ☐	waste ☐

1 buy things on the internet
2 give something to people for money
3 keep money for the future
4 use something that belongs to someone for a short time
5 not use money in a good way

6 have a price
7 give something to someone for a time
8 use money to pay for something
9 give someone the money that they gave you
10 take something back to the store because you don't like it or it isn't right

B ▶ **Now do the vocabulary exercises for 6.1 on page 146.**

C PAIR WORK **Do you waste money on things you don't need? For ideas, watch Allison's video.**

> **!** We can *spend time* or *waste time*.
> *I like to* **spend time** *with my friends.*
> *Don't* **waste your time** *on video games.*

REAL STUDENT

Are you the same as Allison?

3 GRAMMAR: *be going to*

A **Answer the questions. Use the sentences in the grammar box to help you.**

1 Does *going to* describe an action in the past, present, or future? _____

2 When you use *going to*, are you sure about your plans or not? _____

> ### be going to
>
> | | |
> |---|---|
> | This year I**'m going to** buy a TV. | **Are** you **going to** buy that? |
> | We**'re going to** shop online in the future. | We**'re not going to** come back next year. |

B ▶ **Now go to page 134. Look at the grammar chart and do the grammar exercise for 6.1.**

C PAIR WORK **What are <u>you</u> going to do this month? Write four sentences about your plans. Then check your accuracy.**

free time	friends and family	home
study	work	

✓ **ACCURACY** CHECK

When you talk about future plans, remember to use the *-ing* form of *go*.

I ~~go~~ to sell my house. ✗
I'm going to sell my house. ✓

D PAIR WORK **Tell your partner about your plans. Then tell another pair of students about your partner's plans.**

> I'm going to start my new job on Monday.

> Paolo is going to start his new job next week.

4 SPEAKING

A PAIR WORK **Read the ad. Plan a Black Friday shopping trip. Use the words and phrases to help you.**

- When / go?
- What / buy?
- How long / stay there?
- How much / spend?

> When are we going to go?

B **Tell the class about your plans.**

> We're going to go shopping on Friday morning before they sell everything. We're going to buy a flat-screen TV. We're not going to spend over $200.

SHOP THIS WAY

1 VOCABULARY: Shopping

A 🔊 **1.60** PAIR WORK Listen and say the words. Then, with a partner, find the words in the pictures. Write a number in each box. Can you find all of them?

- 1 (shopping) cart
- ☐ cash register
- ☐ checkout
- ☐ customers
- ☐ department store
- ☐ grocery store
- ☐ price
- ☐ sale
- ☐ salesperson
- ☐ shelf

B ▶ Now do the vocabulary exercises for 6.2 on page 146.

C PAIR WORK Make notes about a recent shopping trip. How many words from exercise 1A can you use? Tell your partner about it.

2 LANGUAGE IN CONTEXT

A PAIR WORK Think of a time you bought something you didn't need. Why did you buy it?

B Read the blog post. Find three things that stores do to make us buy more things.

● ● ● ‹ › 🔍 🏠

Never go to the ***grocery store*** *when you're hungry!*

I go grocery shopping most weekends, but I don't like it. I go early, and I don't waste time. But today I went after work to get some eggs for dinner. Big mistake!

When I walked in, I turned right, as most people do. Stores always put their sale items to the right. I put some cheese and some meat in my cart because they were on sale. Then I saw the desserts. All of them were on the middle shelf. Did you know that stores put expensive things on the middle shelf because that's where customers look first? I put two desserts into my cart. Then I smelled the bread. Stores know that fresh bread makes people hungry. Yep, I bought bread, too. I now had many items in my cart! On the way to the checkout, I counted 12 things but no eggs. EGGS! I almost forgot. I went to the egg shelf, but there were none left!

C PAIR WORK What are your shopping habits? Tell your partner.

3 GRAMMAR: Determiners

A (Circle) the correct options to complete the rules. Use the sentences in the grammar box to help you.

1 After determiners like *no*, *some*, and *many*, we use a **singular / plural** noun. This is when we want to talk about **specific things / things in general**.

2 We use a determiner + *of* + *the* + plural noun/object pronoun (*you, us, them*) when we want to talk about **specific things / things in general**.

Determiners

I go grocery shopping **most** weekends.   I now had **many** items in my cart.

I went after work to get **some** eggs for dinner.   I counted 12 things, but **no** eggs.

All of them were on the middle shelf.   There were **none** left.

B **Look at the bold words in the box above. Write them in the correct order below.**

none/no ➡ _____ ➡ _____ ➡ _____ ➡ _____
0%   100%

C ▶ **Now go to page 135. Look at the grammar chart and do the grammar exercise for 6.2.**

D [PAIR WORK] **Write sentences about the stores in your town. Use** *all*, *most*, *many*, *some*, *none*, **or** *no*. **Tell your partner. Do you both agree?**

! *no* or *none*?
no customers
none of the customers

4 SPEAKING

A [GROUP WORK] **Look at the customer survey. Ask your classmates the questions and make notes about their answers.**

B **Share what you learned in exercise 4A.**

Most of the students in this class …

Some of us … .

None of us … .

HELP US | **HELP YOU**

We want to know about our customers.

🛍 Do you prefer shopping with a friend or alone? Why?

🛍 Do you always wait for things to go on sale? Why or why not?

🛍 What's your favorite place to go shopping? Why?

🛍 What is one thing you don't like about shopping? Why?

WHAT DO YOU CALL THEM IN ENGLISH?

LESSON OBJECTIVE
- describe what you want in a store

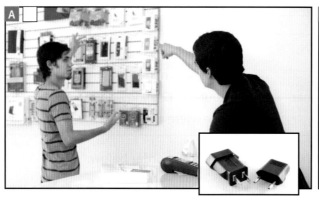
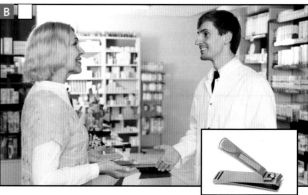

1 FUNCTIONAL LANGUAGE

A Look at the pictures. What type of store are the two customers in?

B 🔊 **1.61** Read and listen to the two conversations. What do the two people buy? Match each conversation to a picture.

> **INSIDER** ENGLISH
>
> Use *get* as another way to say *I understand*.

🔊 **1.61 Audio script**

1 **A** Hi, how can I help you?

B Hello. I'm looking for some things. **You cut your nails with them**.

A What? Oh, you mean "scissors"?

B No. **They're like** scissors, but they're just for nails.

A Oh, got it. Yes, we have them. Nail clippers.

B **What do you call them in English?**

A Nail clippers.

2 **A** Hi there. Can I help you?

B Hello. I'm looking for … um … **I don't know the word** in English. **It's a thing for** my phone.

A A cable?

B No. **You use it to** connect the power cord to the electricity when you're in another country.

A Mm … Oh, I get it! There's one over there. That works for all countries.

B Thanks. **How do you say that in English?**

A It's an adapter. A universal adapter.

C Complete the chart with expressions in **bold** from the conversations above.

Explaining your language problem	Explaining the function of the thing you want
I don't know ¹_____ _____ in English.	²_____ (cut your nails) ³_____ it/them. ⁴_____ it/them ⁵_____ (connect the power cord). They're/It's ⁶_____ (scissors), but … . It's ⁷_____ (my phone).

D PAIR WORK Practice the conversations in exercise 1B with your partner.

2 REAL-WORLD STRATEGY

ASKING FOR WORDS IN ENGLISH

When you want to know a new word, you can ask how to say it in English.

What do you call it/them in English?
How do you say that in English?
What's the English word for … ?

A 🔊 **1.62** **Read about how to ask for words in English in the box above. Then listen to another conversation in a shop. What does the person buy? Which question from the box does he use?**

B 🔊 **1.63** **Read the short conversation. What <u>do</u> you call it in English? Listen and check.**

  A You use it at the supermarket to carry the things you want to buy.

  B Oh, yeah, got it. It's a thing for your groceries. You push it. But what do you call it in English?

  A It's a …

FIND IT

C PAIR WORK **Find three things in the classroom or in your bag that you don't know how to say in English. Use a dictionary or your phone to find the words in English. Have short conversations with your partner like the one in exercise 2B.**

3 PRONUNCIATION: Stressing important words

A 🔊 **1.64** **Listen to the conversation. Notice that important words (usually nouns, verbs, adjectives, or adverbs) are stressed (they're louder and clearer).**

  A <u>What</u>? Oh, you mean <u>scissors</u>?

  B <u>No</u>. They're <u>like</u> scissors, but they're <u>just</u> for <u>nails</u>.

B 🔊 **1.65** <u>Underline</u> **the important words in the conversation below. Then listen. Do the speakers stress the words you underlined? Practice saying the sentences.**

  A I'm looking for something for my phone.

  B A phone charger?

  A No. You use it to connect your phone to electricity.

  B A power cord!

4 SPEAKING

PAIR WORK **Student A: Go to page 158.**
Student B: Go to page 160. Follow
the instructions.

MONEY LESSONS

1 LISTENING

A **PAIR WORK** Think of someone you know who gives good money advice. What advice does he/she give you? Tell a partner.

B **PREDICT** You're going to listen to three stories about problems with money. Look at the pictures. Where do the three stories happen?

A  B  C

C 🔊 **1.66** Listen to the stories. Match the stories (1–3) to the pictures (A–C). Were your answers in exercise 1B correct?

D 🔊 **1.66** **LISTEN FOR DETAIL** Listen to the podcast again. Check (✓) the sentences that are true. Correct the false ones.

____ **1** The women spent many hours drinking tea.

____ **2** The women borrowed some money from a man in the café.

____ **3** Rosa had $60 in her bag when she was in the taxi.

____ **4** The money was still in her bag when she got it back.

____ **5** Senator Richard Burr didn't want people to see him enter his PIN.

____ **6** The Senator left his cash in the ATM.

E **THINK CRITICALLY** **PAIR WORK** Look at the three money lessons the speakers learned. Which lesson do you agree most with? Explain your answer.

■ Some things are more important than money.

■ Pay attention when you're at the ATM.

■ When you travel, check that the banks are open.

2 PRONUNCIATION: Listening for weak words

A 🔊 **1.67** Listen to the sentences from the stories. Circle the words that aren't stressed.

It was the long New Year's weekend a couple of years ago.

None of their ATM cards worked in Japan.

B 🔊 **1.68** **PAIR WORK** Listen and write in the missing words. Compare with a partner.

1 What did you _____ the movie last night?

2 I'm all _____ cash.

C **Complete the sentence.**

A weak form of the word _____ is often used when it's between other words.

3 WRITING

A Read the advice website on how to save money. How many of the suggestions do you agree with?

Top tips to save money
– spending less on the little things in life.

1 One in, one out. When you buy a new shirt, sell or give away an old **one**.

2 Going to the movies? Don't buy snacks at the theater. Go to a store to buy **them** before you go.

3 A "2-for-1" deal isn't always a *good* deal. When a store offers two big bags of chips for $5.00, and a single bag is $3.00, you save $1.00, and that's great! Or is it? If you didn't need all those chips, then you paid $2.00 for something that you didn't really want.

4 Better to borrow than buy. If you only need to wear something once – for example, a suit for a job interview – ask a friend to lend you one.

5 Don't join a gym! If you're going to exercise just once a week, don't waste money on an annual subscription. It's usually cheaper to pay for each fitness class.

6 Go grocery shopping in the evening. That's when supermarkets have sales on many items, and you can fill your cart with more for less!

GLOSSARY
give away (*v*) give something to someone and not ask for money
snack (*n*) a small amount of food between meals
subscription (*n*) money that you pay regularly for a service

B With a partner, decide if the suggestions in exercise 3A are about clothes (C), free time (FT), or shopping (S). Then add two more suggestions for each one.

C **WRITING SKILLS** Look at the words in **bold** in the website. Underline the word in each sentence that *one* and *them* refer to. Find the other example of *one* in the website and underline the word it refers to.

D Rewrite the sentences with the words in parentheses ( ).
1 If you want a new sweater, you can probably find a new sweater in the sale section for less than full price. (one)
2 If you have some pants or a shirt that you didn't wear last year, you're probably not going to wear the pants or shirt this year, either. (them)

WRITE IT

E Imagine you have a vlog. In today's vlog, you are going to make suggestions for saving money on the two topics below. Write your script. Don't forget to use *one* and *them* when you can.
   phone   transportation

F Work with a partner and film your vlog. Watch the vlogs in class and say what the best advice is.

TIME TO SPEAK
Eureka!

A Look at the ideas in the photos with a partner. What are they for? Why are they useful?

folding bicycle

B The best ideas help solve a problem. With a partner, match the ideas in exercise A with the problems they help solve.

1 VR headsets are very expensive. ____
2 My bicycle is too big to fit on the bus or train. ____
3 Bananas become soft and brown in my bag. ____
4 Baby strollers are heavy and slow. ____

banana protector

C DISCUSS Here are more problems. Think of an idea to help solve them. Be creative! Use the phrases at the bottom of the page to help you.

- I often forget where I put my phone.
- Grocery bags full of food are really heavy, and they sometimes break.
- I hate my alarm clock. It's so loud, and I wake up tired and unhappy.
- My dog needs more exercise, but I don't have time in the evenings for a walk.
- I need somewhere to put my cold drink when I'm at the beach.

cardboard VR headset
(VR = Virtual Reality)

INVENTORS WANTED!

Do you have an **amazing idea** for a **new invention?** We want to buy it!

Tell us about your idea. We want to know:
> what are you going to call your invention?
> how is it going to work?
> what problem is it going to solve?
> how much is it going to cost?
> who is going to buy it?

longboard baby stroller

D PREPARE Read the announcement above. You are going to present one of your ideas from exercise C. Discuss the questions in the announcement to help you prepare your presentation.

E PRESENT Present your invention to the class. Listen to the other presentations and ask questions about their ideas.

F Imagine you and your group are business experts. You have $5,000. You can give this all to one group, or share it between different groups. Talk about the ideas you thought were good. Who are you going to give the money to, and why?

To check your progress, go to page 154.

USEFUL PHRASES

DISCUSS
Maybe a … / What about a …
… would be useful.
I have an idea for a …
That sounds great!
I love that idea!

PREPARE
My favorite idea was …
Who's going to talk about … ?

PRESENT
We're going to tell you about our new idea …
People are going to love it because …
It's really simple/useful/ fun.
We think it's going to make lots of money.

REVIEW 2 (UNITS 4–6)

1 VOCABULARY

A   Look at the word cloud. Find five words or phrases for each category below.

fun candle department store **amazing musician**
grocery store **borrow** graduate from college **retire** bouquet of flowers
candy **perfume** get married jewelry **crazy**
artist **cool actor** cost
have a baby **buy a house** **checkout singer** spend
shelf **sale** strange director lend
save

1 pop culture: *actor,* _____	4 life events: _____
2 gifts: _____	5 using money: _____
3 opinions: _____	6 shopping: _____

B   Add three more words or phrases that you know to each category.

2 GRAMMAR

A   Complete the sentences with the present continuous or simple past of the verbs in parentheses ( ).
Then find the object pronouns (*you*, *me*, *us*, etc.) and ⃝circle them. What nouns do they replace?
Underline them.

1   My father _____ (retire) next week. His coworkers _____ (plan) a party for him.

2   My best friend _____ (start) her new job last Monday.

3   My sister _____ (get) married next Saturday. We're all very excited!

4   Yesterday _____ (be) my neighbor's 75th birthday. I _____ (not go) to his party
    because I _____ (not be) home.

5   My boss and her family _____ (move) to their new house next month. We should buy her
    a gift.

6   My cousin and her husband _____ (have) a baby two weeks ago. I'm so happy for them.

B   PAIR WORK   Write five sentences about big events in your life and the lives of people you know using
the present continuous and simple past. Read your sentences with a partner.

C   Look at the sentences you wrote in 2B again. Are your object pronouns correct? Underline the nouns
that your object pronouns replace to check. Correct your work.

3 SPEAKING

PAIR WORK   You need to buy a gift for each of the people in Grammar exercise 2A. Answer the
questions.

■   What are you going to buy?
■   Where are you going to buy it?
■   How much are you going to spend?

> I'm going to buy my grandfather a book about
> boats. He loves boats. I'm going to buy it online.
> I'm not going to spend more than $30.

4 FUNCTIONAL LANGUAGE

A **Use the words and phrases in the box to complete the conversation.**

congratulations	I can't	love to	meet
sorry to hear	too bad	we're going	would you like

A Hey, guess what? I got the job!

B Wow, that's great! ¹_____!

A Thanks! ²_____ to come out and celebrate with us? ³_____ bowling and then getting pizza.

B I'd really ⁴_____, but ⁵_____. I failed one of my tests last week, and I need to take it again on Monday. So I'm studying the whole weekend.

A Oh no, that's ⁶_____. I'm really ⁷_____ that. Maybe you could only come out for pizza, then. Just for an hour? Come on! You need to eat.

B Oh, OK. Where are you going?

A Great! Let's ⁸_____ at Dom's Pizza at eight. See you there!

B **Read the sentences. Can you guess what it is?**

1 I'm looking for a bag to hold money and other things. I don't know the word in English.

2 I'm looking for a thing for my phone, for the battery. I don't know how to say it in English.

3 I don't know the word in English, but it's something for my groceries. I mean, you use it to put food in when you go around the grocery store.

5 SPEAKING

A **PAIR WORK** **Choose one of the situations below. Act it out in pairs.**

1 Imagine it's your birthday tomorrow. Decide what you're going to do, where you're going to go, and when. Call a friend to ask them to come to your party.

   A Hey, tomorrow's my birthday, and I'm …

   B Oh, I wish I could …

2 Imagine your friend passed her driving test. Call your friend to congratulate her. Suggest doing something together to celebrate.

   A I just heard that you passed your driving test!

   B Yeah! I'm so excited!

3 You want to buy a gift for a friend. First decide what you want to buy. Then imagine you're in a store. Ask the clerk to help you. You don't know the word in English.

   A May I help you?

   B Hi, yes, I'm looking for …

B **Change roles and repeat the role play.**

GRAMMAR REFERENCE AND PRACTICE

1.1 *BE*; POSSESSIVE ADJECTIVES (page 3)

be

	Affirmative	Negative	Question	Short answers
I	**am** from Indiana.	**'m not** from Florida.	**Am** I late?	Yes, I **am**. No, I **'m not**.
He / She / It	**is** my roommate.	**'s not** my boyfriend.	**Is** he/she/it from Indiana?	Yes, he **is**. No, he **isn't**.
You / We / They	**are** close friends.	**'re not** close friends.	**Are** they your neighbors?	Yes, they **are**. No, they're **not**.

A Complete the sentences with the correct verb or possessive adjective. Use contractions where possible.

!	People usually say:	You can also say:
	you're not	*you aren't*
	we're not	*we aren't*
	they're not	*he/she/it isn't*
	he's/she's/it's not	*he/she/it isn't*

1 We 're _____ students. _____ names are Marc and Belinda.
2 He _____ from Scotland. _____ name is Ron.
3 I _____ Colombian, but _____ mother is from Brazil.
4 They _____ in the classroom. _____ teacher is Emily.
5 _____ name is Mr. Brinkley. He _____ the boss.
6 My city _____ famous for _____ tacos.

1.2 POSSESSION (page 5)

Possession (pages 3 and 5)

Subject pronouns	Possessive adjectives		Possessive pronouns	
I	**my**	It's **my** mirror.	**mine**	It's **mine**.
you	**your**	It's **your** bottle.	**yours**	It's **yours**.
he	**his**	It's **his** brush.	**his**	It's **his**.
she	**her**	It's **her** gum.	**hers**	It's **hers**.
we	**our**	It's **our** house.	**ours**	It's **ours**.
they	**their**	It's **their** umbrella.	**theirs**	It's **theirs**.
Use *whose* to ask about possession.		*Whose* is this? *Whose* bag is this? It's mine.		
We can also say		*Who* does this (bag) **belong to**? It's mine. / It belongs to me.		
's shows possession		my son**'s** keychain (= the keychain that belongs to my son)		

A **Circle** the correct options to complete the conversations.

1 A *Who's / Whose* car is that?

  B It's not *our / ours*.

2 A *Who / Whose* does this cash belong to? Is it *your / yours*?

  B No. It's *mine / my sister's*.

3 A Whose hairbrush *is this / does this belong to*?

  B It's *my mother's / of my mother*.

4 A Hey! That's *mine / my*.

  B No, it isn't. It *belongs / is* to me.

5 A Is this *your / yours* umbrella?

  B No, it's *Donna / Donna's*. *Mine / My* is red.

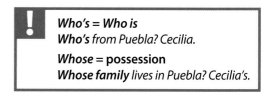

! *Who's = Who is*
Who's from Puebla? Cecilia.

Whose = possession
Whose family lives in Puebla? Cecilia's.

2.1 SIMPLE PRESENT FOR HABITS AND ROUTINES (page 13)

Simple present for habits and routines

	Affirmative	Negative	Question	Short answers
I	**sleep** for eight hours.	**don't sleep** much.		
He / She / It	**sleeps** for six hours.	**doesn't sleep** much.	**Does** she **sleep** a lot?	Yes, she **does**. No, he **doesn't**.
You / We / They	**sleep** for seven hours.	**don't sleep** much.	**Do** you **sleep** a lot?	Yes, we **do**. No, they **don't**.

Information questions

Where does he **study**?

Why do we **have** homework?

How do they **get** to and from work?

How many hours **do** you **sleep** a night?

Time phrases

Every day/evening/week/month

On Monday/the weekend

In the morning/the afternoon/ the evening

A **Use the words to write simple present sentences.**

1 A What time / your daughter / get up / on the weekend?

   What time does your daughter get up on the weekend?

  B She / usually / get up / very late.

_____

2 A How often / you / ride to work / together?

_____

  B We / always / ride to work together, / but / Laura / not drive.

_____

3 A How often / watch TV / on the weekend?

_____

  B I / not / watch TV / on the weekend. I / watch TV / every evening after work.

_____

2.2 *THIS / THAT ONE; THESE / THOSE ONES* (page 15)

A (Circle) the correct words to complete the sentences. Then match the questions (1–6)
and the answers (a–f).

1 Is *these / this / those* your coffee? ___	**a** That *one / ones* costs $245.
2 Can I use *that / these / those* outlet, please? ___	**b** Then use these *one / ones*.
3 *That / This / Those* headphones don't work. ___	**c** Yes, they are.
4 Are *that / this / those* your notes? ___	**d** No, that *one / ones* is my coffee.
5 What's *that / these / this* over there? ___	**e** No, please use that *one / ones*.
6 How much does *that / these / those* phone cost? ___	**f** I don't know what *that / these / those* is.

3.1 PRESENT CONTINUOUS (page 23)

Present continuous

	Affirmative	Negative	Question	Short answers
I	**'m winning.**	**'m not watching** the game.		
You / We / They	**'re going** to the gym.	**'re not playing** well.	**Are** they **winning**?	Yes, they **are**. No, they **aren't**.
He / She / It	**'s losing.**	**'s not having** a good game.	**Is** it **raining**?	Yes, it **is**. No, it **isn't**.

A **Complete the live-feed events with the present continuous of the verbs in parentheses.**

The swimmers [1] _____ *are coming* _____ (come) in now. They
[2] _____ (wait) for the start. The champion
[3] _____ (look) at the fans, but she
[4] _____ (not smile). She has her headphones
on – what music [5] _____ (she listen) to?

SPORTS LIVE

B **Use the words to write sentences. Use the present continuous of the verbs.**

1 The people / leave / the stadium

2 The drivers / start / their engines

3 What / the coach / do?

4 It / rain / but / the runners / not stop

5 The winner / smile / and / cry

6 My favorite player / not win / any games at the moment

7 He / run / with the ball

8 The fans / wear / team hats

3.2 SIMPLE PRESENT AND PRESENT CONTINUOUS (page 25)

A Read the conversations. Complete the sentences with the simple present or present continuous of the verbs in parentheses.

1 A What _____ (you / do)?

 B I'm waiting for my friend.

2 A Does he go to a gym?

 B Yes, _____ (do).

3 A Can you talk now?

 B No, I can't. I _____ (drive).

4 A You _____ (not / listen) to me!

 B Sorry, I _____ (watch) the game.

5 A What _____ (you / read)?

 B It's a book about exercise.

6 A Mom! Ben _____ (kick) me again!

 B Stop it, Ben!

7 A Why _____ (you / lie down)?

 B Because I'm tired.

8 A Hurry! The game starts in two minutes.

 B I _____ (come)!

4.1 PRESENT CONTINUOUS FOR FUTURE PLANS (page 35)

Present continuous for future plans			
Affirmative	**Negative**	**Question**	**Information question**
Comic Con **is coming** here this weekend.	He **isn't selling** anything.	**Are** you **going** to Comic Con?	What **are** you **doing** later?

A Use the words to write sentences about future plans. Use contractions when you can.

> ! Present continuous for plans usually includes a future time expression.
> *What are you doing **tomorrow**?*
> *We're going to the beach **on the weekend**.*

1 My cousin / play in a concert / next Saturday.

 My cousin's playing in a concert next Saturday.

2 I / go to a concert / with my best friend tonight.

_____

3 you / play video games / with your friends later?

_____

4 We / watch our team / at the stadium on my birthday.

_____

5 We / not go / to the pool today.

_____

6 She / not go to the game / this weekend.

_____

4.2 OBJECT PRONOUNS (page 37)

Subject pronoun	Object pronoun	
I / we	me / us	They buy great gifts for **me** / **us**.
you	you	I'm getting a special gift for **you**.
he / she / they	him / her / them	I'm seeing **him** / **her** / **them** tomorrow.
it	it	This is a great gift! I love **it**!

A (Circle) the correct options to complete the conversations.

1 **A** We're having a party on Saturday. Do you think John would like to come?

    B Why don't you ask *her / him / me*?

2 **A** My grandparents are visiting us right now.

    B Oh yeah? Please say hello to *him / us / them* for me!

3 **A** Is your brother coming to my party this weekend?

    B Yes, he is. And he's bringing a special gift for *him / it / you*.

4 **A** Do you like soccer?

    B Do I like soccer? I love *them / you / it*!

5 **A** My mom is starting a new job next week.

    B Really? Tell *her / him / you* good luck!

6 **A** Can I ask *her / us / you* a question?

    B Yeah, sure thing. What do you want to ask?

5.1 SIMPLE PAST (page 45)

Simple past of *be*

	Affirmative	Negative	Question	Short answers
I / He / She / It	**was** cool.	**wasn't** loud.	**Was** it fun?	Yes, it **was**. / No, it **wasn't**.
You / We / They	**were** perfect.	**weren't** proud.	**Were** they crazy?	Yes, they **were**. / No, they **weren't**.

Simple past

Regular verbs: verb + -(e)d		Irregular verbs	
learn → learn**ed**	love → lov**ed**	do → **did**	have → **had**
visit → visit**ed**	study → stud**ied**	go → **went**	hit → **hit**

A **Complete the texts with the simple past of the verbs in the box.**

> arrive ~~be~~ hate miss not remember walk want

I remember my first day of school. It ¹_____*was*_____ just horrible!
I ²_____ every minute of it! My older sister ³_____ with me,
but she ⁴_____ the way, so we got lost. Finally, we ⁵_____ ,
but we were very late. I really ⁶_____ my mom and dad. All day, I just
⁷_____ to go home.

5.2 SIMPLE PAST NEGATIVE AND QUESTIONS (page 47)

Simple past negative and questions

	Affirmative	Negative	Question	Short answers
I / He / She / It / You / We / They	**studied** medicine.	**didn't study** journalism.	**Did** he **study** medicine?	Yes, he **did.** No, she **didn't.**

Information questions	
What did you **study?**	**Why did** she **retire?**
When did they **get** married?	**Who did** you **live** with?
Where did he **come** from?	**How many children did** they **have?**

A **Use the words to write questions about when your partner was a child. Ask and answer the questions in pairs.**

1 What / eat?

_____

2 Where / live?

_____

3 When / start school?

_____

4 What / watch on TV?

_____

5 What games / play?

_____

6.1 *BE GOING TO* (page 55)

be going to + verb

	Affirmative	Negative	Question	Short answers
I	**am/'m going to save** money for a new bike.	**am/'m not going to waste** money.	**Am** I **going to save** money?	Yes, I **am.** No, I**'m not.**
He / She / It	**is/'s going to buy** her mom a birthday present at the mall.	**is/'s not going to see** the movie with us.	**Is** she **going to sell** some of her old clothes online?	Yes, she **is.** No, she **isn't.**
You / We / They	**are/'re going to do** a lot today.	**are/'re not going to save** money.	**Are** they **going to shop** online?	Yes, they **are.** No, they **aren't.**

Information questions
Who am I **going to go** shopping with?
What is she **going to buy?**
Where are you **going to meet** them for lunch?

A   **Complete the sentences with the correct form of *be going to* and one of the verbs in the box.**

| buy | ~~come~~ | get married | have | lie down | not have |

1   The big sale starts tomorrow. _____*Are*_____ you _____*going to come*_____ with us?
2   I'm tired after all this shopping. I _____ for a while.
3   We met at the grocery store, and fell in love. We _____ in November.
4   I'm working all day Black Friday. I _____ time to buy anything!
5   My brother is buying baby clothes. His wife _____ a baby in three months.
6   You found the car you want already? When _____ you _____ it?

6.2   DETERMINERS (page 57)

Determiners		
Things or people in general	**Specific things or people**	**With pronouns**
All sales clerks are friendly. (= sales clerks in general)	**All (of) the** sales clerks here are friendly. (= the sales clerks in this store specifically)	**All of us/them** …
Most stores have good sales on Black Friday.	**Most of the** stores in town have good sales on Black Friday.	**Most of them** …
Many stores are in shopping malls.	**Many of the** stores in this mall are expensive.	**Many of them** …
Some people don't like shopping.	**Some of the** people in my family don't like shopping.	**Some of us** …
No customers like high prices.	**None of the** customers who shop here like high prices.	**None of us/them** …

A   **Circle the correct words to complete the sentences.**

1   *Many of / Many* the good stores in my town are at the mall.
2   *Most / None* stores have special carts for young children.
3   On the day before a big holiday, *none / all* the lines at the grocery stores are very long.
4   *None of / Some* prices in grocery stores are better at the end of the day.
5   *Many of / None* the stores have sale ads in their windows.

This page is intentionally left blank

VOCABULARY PRACTICE

1.1 PEOPLE YOU KNOW (page 2)

A **Put the words into the right category.**

boss	boyfriend	classmate	close friend	couple	girlfriend
grandchildren	granddaughter	grandson	neighbor	roommate	

Family	Work or school	Close or romantic	Where you live

B **Complete the sentences with the correct form of the words from exercise A.**

1 She is not my sister. She is my brother's _____. They are in love.

2 My grandfather has five other _____: my two sisters and my three cousins.

3 Kevin and Paola are my _____ at the language school. They're also a _____, but they're not married.

4 Fiona and I are _____ from work. We do a lot of things together in our free time.

5 Isabel is only 45, but she is already a grandmother. Her _____, Jazmin, is two years old. She is the daughter of Isabel's son, Oscar.

6 I have a job in a restaurant, and my _____ is also my _____. My apartment is #302. He is in apartment #304.

7 I have two _____. We each have one bedroom in the apartment, but we share the kitchen.

1.2 NAMING EVERYDAY THINGS (page 4)

A **Check (✓) the words that you can see in the pictures.**

| 1 | 2 | 3 | 4 | 5 | 6 |

- [ ] candy bar
- [ ] cash
- [ ] driver's license
- [ ] gum
- [ ] hairbrush
- [ ] hand lotion
- [ ] keychain
- [ ] mirror
- [ ] receipt
- [ ] tissues
- [ ] umbrella
- [ ] water bottle

B **Circle the correct words to complete the sentences.**

1 There is a photo of me on my *driver's license / mirror*.

2 My *cash / water bottle* is empty.

3 Here is the *tissues / receipt* from the restaurant.

4 Do you want a piece of my *candy bar / hairbrush*?

5 Oh, no! It's raining, and my *hand lotion / umbrella* is broken.

6 I need to clean my sunglasses. Will you give me those *tissues / keychains*, please?

2.1 EXPRESSIONS WITH *DO, HAVE,* AND *MAKE* (page 12)

A   (Circle) the correct words to complete the sentences.

1   I *do / have / make* a lot of work on my laptop every day.

2   I want to *do / have / make* a party when we *do / have / make* some free time.

3   I usually *do / have / make* the dishes, but I don't *do / have / make* other housework.

4   I always *do / have / make* a snack after I *do / have / make* one hour of homework.

5   I want to *do / have / make* plans with some friends, maybe just *do / have / make* something to drink after class.

B   Complete the sentences with the correct *do, have,* or *make* phrase.

1   Lots of men don't _____ *do housework* _____ , but not my sons. They
_____ after they wake up, and they _____ when
their clothes are dirty.

2   Can we _____ now? I'm hungry.

3   I'm tired of walking. I want to stop and _____ at that café.

4   I want to _____ for my birthday party. Can you help me organize it?

5   I always _____ after dinner. I like the kitchen to be clean before I go to bed.

6   Let's go to the movies when you _____ – maybe this weekend!

2.2 NAMING WORK AND STUDY ITEMS (page 14)

A   Match the words on the left to the words on the right to make phrases. Then write full sentences using the phrases.

(1) a page from	(a) a calendar
(2) music	(b) a textbook
(3) a laptop	(c) files
(4) take	(d) notes
(5) the date on	(e) screen

(6) wear	(f) a document
(7) a computer	(g) headphones
(8) a power	(h) keyboard
(9) read	(i) outlet
(10) free	(j) Wi-Fi

I'm reading a page from my textbook.

B   (Circle) the correct words to complete the questions. Then ask a partner.

1   Does your school have good *document / Wi-Fi* and enough *screens / outlets* for all the students' computers?

2   Do you like to listen to music with or without your *headphones / keyboard*?

3   Can you always find your *documents / mouse* and *files / Wi-Fi* on your computer?

4   Do you write important things on your *calendar / keyboard*?

5   Which can you do faster, write *files / notes* with a pen and paper or type them on a *keyboard / mouse*?

3.1 SPORTS (page 22)

A   (Circle) the correct words to complete the sentences.

1   Our *coach / court* is happy because we're *losing / winning*.

2   Our *fans / team* is *losing / winning* the game. This is terrible!

3   The *field / players* are walking onto the *court / pool* now.

4   Our town has a new *coach / pool*. It's next to the tennis *players / courts*.

5   Hundreds of *fans / team* are running onto the *field / pool*.

B **Complete the sentences with the correct form of a word from exercise A.**

1 The first _____ to _____ the FIFA World Cup was Uruguay.

2 An Olympic swimming _____ is 50 meters long, and a basketball _____ is 92 meters long.

3 The soccer _____ is giving instructions. He's at the side of the _____.

4 This place is huge! It has seats for more than 100,000 _____.

5 The _____ on my local team are not professionals, and they aren't very good – they often _____ games.

3.2 EXERCISING (page 25)

A **Match the verbs in the box to the words that can follow them.**

climb	jump	lie down	lift	push
sit down	stand up	stretch	throw	~~turn~~

1 _____turn_____ around / your head

2 _____ a ball / a paper plane

3 _____ someone away / an elevator button

4 _____ a mountain / stairs

5 _____ a box / weights

6 _____ to rest / on the floor

7 _____ at your desk / in front of the TV

8 _____ your legs before you run / to reach something high up

9 _____ into the water / up and down

10 _____ from your desk / straight

B **Complete the sentences with a word from exercise A.**

1 A good baseball player can _____ a ball more than 130 meters.

2 Some people can _____ more than 6 meters on a trampoline.

3 Some people can _____ 200 kilograms.

4 A very good dancer can _____ a full circle in the air twice.

5 Most people need two months to _____ Mount Everest.

6 For some exercises, you need to _____ on the floor.

7 Before you play any sports, it's important to _____ your arms and legs.

4.1 DESCRIBING POP CULTURE (page 34)

A **Some of the words in bold are not correct. Write in the correct words.**

> band

1 My sister is a **singer** in a ~~musician~~. They're playing a **concert** tonight.

2 My favorite **TV show** is coming back soon. I love the main **director** in it – he's so funny!

3 Do you know about this new **festival**? It's fantastic! I'm playing it eight hours a day!

4 The **actor** who paints these pictures is very famous. I saw her work at an **concert** in Paris.

B **Complete the stories with the words in the box.**

bands	concerts	festival	musicians

Every year in my town we have a three-day music ¹_____.
There are ²_____ every night, and all the ³_____
play until late. The ⁴_____ are all local people, and everybody
in the town goes to see them. Would you like to come with me this year?

actor	artist	director	show	singer	video

My family is very artistic. My mom is a great ⁵_____ – she sings
in a band. My uncle is an ⁶_____. He's starring in a cool TV
⁷_____ right now. My brother is an ⁸_____. He
does the graphics for lots of ⁹_____ games. And my dad's a
movie ¹⁰_____. He makes great movies. I'm the only one who
isn't artistic, but I'm the manager for all my relatives!

4.2 NAMING GIFT ITEMS (page 36)

A **What gift is best for each person?**

candy	gift card	jewelry	purse	speakers	sweatshirt

1 I want something beautiful to wear to parties. _____
2 I prefer to buy my own present in the store. _____
3 I'd like something to wear at the gym. _____
4 I'd like something nice to keep my things in. _____
5 I like music. _____
6 I love sweet things to eat. _____

B Circle the correct words to complete the sentences.

1 My grandma likes gifts that she can eat, so I usually make a cake or buy some *flowers / candy* for her.
2 My mom really needs GPS when she drives, but that uses a lot of battery power. So I'm getting her *speakers / a phone charger* for her car.
3 My dad loves sports clothes, so I'm buying him a *sweatshirt / purse.*
4 My best friend loves books, but I don't know which ones she likes. I'm getting her a *purse / gift card* for the bookstore so she can choose.
5 I don't know what to get for my boss for her birthday, so I'm sending her *a bouquet of flowers / jewelry.*

5.1 DESCRIBING OPINIONS AND FEELINGS (page 45)

A **Replace the emoji in each sentence with the correct adjective.**

1 My first day in college was really ___horrible___ 😖. I felt very alone, and I missed my parents.

2 My 18th birthday was an _____ 🙂 experience – for the first time, I was an adult!

3 I remember the first day I went skiing. It was really _____ 😃 . My friends and I had a great time.

4 The first time that I voted was a very _____ 😌 moment for me. It was an important day for my country, and I was part of it.

5 I remember when I traveled by plane for the first time. That was _____ 🙃 ! Wow!

B **Complete the conversations with the words from the box. Write two more conversations using other words from the box.**

angry	cool	crazy	dangerous	loud	perfect	tired

1 **A** How are you feeling today?

   B I'm really _____ . I went to bed very late last night.

2 **A** Do you like this music?

   B What? I can't hear you. It's really _____ !

3 **A** How was your vacation?

   B It was _____ ! The weather was great, and the food was delicious.

4 **A** _____

   B _____

5 **A** _____

   B _____

5.2 DESCRIBING LIFE EVENTS (page 46)

A **Complete the sentences with the correct word or phrase from the box.**

buy a house or apartment	get married	graduate from college
learn to drive	meet your future husband/wife	retire

1 These days, people often _____ quite late, when they are 30 or 40 years old.

2 Today, it's important to _____ because you have more choices for work.

3 Some people _____ at the usual time (around age 65), but some work until they are 75 or older.

4 Some young people don't have the money to _____ right away. They stay with their parents until they have enough money.

5 You can't really plan when to _____ . One day, it just happens – you just find the right person.

B **Circle the best phrase to complete the sentences.**

1 My mother has three children, and someday she really wants to *become a grandparent / have a baby*.

2 If you want to *buy a car / learn to drive*, you need to *get a job / get married* and save some money first.

3 My little brother *had a baby / was born* when I was seven, so I helped take care of him. He was so cute!

4 For some jobs, you have to *graduate from college / start school*.

5 She *got married / met her future husband* at the coffee shop where she worked. He got coffee there every day just to talk to her. After they *got married / bought a car*, he told her that he doesn't like coffee.

6 My sister's son *started school / were born* last year, so she has some free time now. She wants to *get a job / retire* soon.

6.1 USING MONEY (page 54)

A **Circle the correct word to complete the sentences.**

1 David wants to buy a car, so he *saves / spends* a lot of his money.

2 Jamelia is very careful. She never *wastes / sells* money on silly things.

3 My friend wants to *spend / borrow* some money from me.

4 I don't like to buy things in stores because it's more fun to *lend / shop* online.

5 Be careful! That phone *costs / pays back* a lot of money!

6 Our store always *borrows / sells* a lot on Black Friday.

B **Complete the questions with the correct form of a verb from exercise A.**

1 Excuse me, how much does this _____ ?

2 Can I _____ $2.00? I have $10, but I need $12 for the ticket.

3 Where do you like to _____ online?

4 This charger was a gift, but it doesn't work. Can I _____ it without the receipt?

5 If you have enough money, can you _____ me $20? I'll pay you back.

6.2 SHOPPING (page 56)

A **Complete the shopping words.**

1 c _____ re _____ ter

2 c _____ stom _____ rs

3 gro _____ ery st _____ r _____

4 dep _____ rtm _____ nt st _____ r _____

5 she _____ _____

6 s _____ l _____

7 pri _____ e

8 salesp _____ rson

9 ch _____ ck _____ t

10 c _____ r _____

B **Complete the text with words from exercise A.**

Last week, I went to a new ¹ _____ store to buy some milk. It was in the back. I needed to walk down many aisles. In one aisle, they had a really good ² _____ on bottled water, so I decided to buy some. In another aisle, there was some delicious bread. There was some very interesting fruit, fresh fish, and delicious rice in other aisles. Next to the milk, there were amazing cheeses! I walked down most of the aisles in the store. When I got to the ³ _____ , my ⁴ _____ was full. There were three ⁵ _____ in front of me. I waited and read a magazine from the ⁶ _____ . Then I decided to buy it, too.

PROGRESS CHECK

Can you do these things? Check (✓) what you can do. Then write your answers in your notebook.

Now I can …	Prove it	UNIT 1
☐ use words to talk about the people in my life.	Write two family words, two words for people you work or study with, and four other words for people you know.	
☐ talk about the connections between the people in my life.	Write about someone you know and what connection that person has to other people you know using possessive adjectives (*my, our, his*, etc.).	
☐ use words for everyday objects.	Write four things you have with you today and two things you always have in your bag.	
☐ talk about what belongs to me and to others.	Look around the room and write three sentences about objects and who they belong to. Use possessive pronouns (*mine, ours, his*, etc.).	
☐ start a conversation with someone new.	Write three ways to start a conversation.	
☐ write a formal email of introduction.	Look at your email from lesson 1.4, exercise 2D. Can you make it better? Find three ways.	

Now I can …	Prove it	UNIT 2
☐ use expressions with *do, have,* and *make*.	Write five things related to activities at home. Use *do, have,* and *make*.	
☐ talk about what I do every day, on the weekend, etc.	Write five things you do regularly (every day, every week, etc.).	
☐ use words for work and study.	Write a description of the place you do your work and/or schoolwork.	
☐ use *this/that one; these/those ones* to talk about things.	Complete the sentences: *I don't like these shirts. I prefer* _____ _____ *over there.* *That car is OK, but* _____ _____ *is much nicer.*	
☐ describe communication problems and how to fix them.	Write two ways to explain a communication problem and two ways to check the problem.	
☐ write your opinion and give information in an online comment.	Look at your comment from lesson 2.4, exercise 3C. Can you make it better? Find three ways.	

Now I can …	Prove it	UNIT 3
☐ use words to talk about sports.	Write two verbs for sports, three places for sports, and five other sports words.	
☐ talk about what I am doing now.	Write one thing you're doing at the moment and one thing you're not doing at the moment.	
☐ use words to describe exercise.	Write five verbs to describe exercise.	
☐ talk about what I do every day and what I'm doing at the moment.	Complete these sentences: *I usually … At the moment, I …*	
☐ ask for information.	Write two ways to ask for the price of a soccer ticket.	
☐ write a short comment about positives and negatives	Look at your comment from lesson 3.4, exercise 1E. Can you make it better? Find three ways.	

PROGRESS CHECK

Can you do these things? Check (✓) what you can do. Then write your answers in your notebook.

UNIT 4

Now I can …

□ use words to talk about pop culture.

□ talk about plans.

□ use words to talk about gifts.

□ use *him*, *her*, etc. to talk about people and things.

□ make and respond to invitations.

□ write an event announcement.

Prove it

Write five jobs, two special events, and three other words about pop culture.

Write two things you're planning to do on the weekend. Use the present continuous.

Write three gifts you can wear, two you can use, and one you can eat.

Complete these sentences with an object pronoun:
Soccer is his favorite sport. I love … , too.
Their parents always give … money for their birthdays.

Write one way to make an invitation and one way to accept an invitation.

Look at your event announcement from lesson 4.4, exercise 3D. Can you make it better? Find three ways.

UNIT 5

Now I can …

□ use words to talk about feelings and opinions.

□ talk about events and people in my life.

□ talk about life stages.

□ ask questions about people's lives and say what they didn't do.

□ congratulate and sympathize with people.

□ write an online comment agreeing or disagreeing with someone.

Prove it

Write five positive words, three negative words, and two words that can be positive or negative.

Write three things you did last year.

Write six life stages in the order that they usually happen.

Complete the sentences: _____ he retire last year? No, he _____ .

Write two ways to congratulate someone and two ways to sympathize with someone.

Look at your comment from lesson 5.4, exercise 2D. Can you make it better? Find three ways.

UNIT 6

Now I can …

□ use verbs to talk about money.

□ talk about future plans.

□ use words to talk about shopping.

□ talk about quantities of things.

□ say what I want when I do not know the word.

□ write a vlog script.

Prove it

Write three verbs that go with *money*, two verbs that go with *things,* and three other money verbs.

Write about a plan you have for next week and a plan you have for next year. Use *be going to.*

Write three places for shopping and four things you can find in a store.

Complete the sentences: *Many of the stores in my town don't … All department stores sell …*

Think about something you want to buy but you don't know the word for in English. Write a short conversation in a store. Explain what you want.

Look at your vlog script from lesson 6.4, exercise 3E. Can you make it better? Find three ways.

PAIR WORK PRACTICE (STUDENT A)

2.3 EXERCISE 4   STUDENT A

Choose a reason for calling from the list below. Think about what you want to say, and add some detail. Now phone your partner. Use the chart below to help you.

> **Reasons for calling**
> - you're sick
> - there's a problem with the subway, and you're late
> - you want to meet
> - you have a problem you want to talk about

Student A		Student B
Greet B and give a reason for the call.	→	Greet A. Tell A there's a problem.
Try to solve the problem. Ask if it's OK now.	→	It isn't OK now. Ask A for repetition.
Repeat what you said.	→	The problem continues. Suggest a solution.

3.3 EXERCISE 2D   STUDENT A

1   **Ask Student B some questions about the items below using the functional language on page 26. If B doesn't understand the word, explain it with the definitions in parentheses.**

The restroom (*where the public bathrooms are*)

The bleachers (*the cheap seats in a stadium that aren't covered*)

A side of fries (*some fries with your food order*)

2   **Now listen to Student B. If you don't understand a word or words, repeat them as a question. Do you understand the words now?**

5.3 EXERCISE 2C   STUDENT A

1   **Tell your partner what good things happened yesterday. Use these words:**

graduated   new job   house / apartment   car

2   **Now listen to the good things that happened to student B. Congratulate him/her, but check the information he/she gives you*, and offer the correct version using *Do you mean …?* or *You mean …?***

(**Clue: Use the Vocabulary words on page 46 to check.*)

5.5 EXERCISE B   GROUP A

Story A

Eva Hart from the U.K. was only seven years old. She traveled as a second-class passenger with her parents. Her father put Eva and her mother on a lifeboat. He didn't survive. In later years, Eva was very critical of the shipping company – The White Star Line. After the accident, she even wrote an autobiography, *Shadow of the Titanic, A Survivor's Story*.

PAIR WORK PRACTICE

5.5 EXERCISE B   GROUP B

Story B

Molly Brown was a 44-year-old American woman. She was a well-known politician from a rich family. She traveled alone as a first-class passenger. She escaped the sinking ship on a lifeboat. She helped a lot of the survivors on board the *Carpathia*. She became famous because of her bravery and spoke a lot about the tragedy in the years to come.

6.3 EXERCISE 4   STUDENT A

1   **You want to buy something from a drugstore but you don't know the word for it in English. Choose one of the objects below and ask the salesperson for what you want.**

A   B   C   D   E

2   **You are now the sales clerk. Your partner wants to buy something. Begin by asking if you can help.**

PAIR WORK PRACTICE

2.3 EXERCISE 4 STUDENT B

Choose a communication problem from the list below. Think about what you want to say. Now wait for your partner to phone you.

> **Communication problems**
> - echo on the line
> - bad connection
> - traffic or a train noise
> - problem with the Wi-Fi

Student A		**Student B**
Greet B and give a reason for the call.	→	Greet A. Tell A there's a problem.
Try to solve the problem. Ask if it's OK now.	→	It isn't OK now. Ask A for repetition.
Repeat what you said.	→	The problem continues. Suggest a solution.

3.3 EXERCISE 2D STUDENT B

1 **Listen to Student A. If you don't understand a word or words, repeat them as a question. Do you understand the words now?**

2 **Now ask Student A some questions about the items below using the functional language on page 26. If A doesn't understand the word, explain it with the definitions in parentheses.**

   The parking lot (*where you park your car*)

   Baseball cap (*the hat baseball players and fans wear*)

   A noise maker (*something you use to make lots of noise in the game*)

5.3 EXERCISE 2C STUDENT B

1 **Listen to the good things that happened to student A. Congratulate him/her, but check the information he/she gives you*, and offer the correct version using *Do you mean … ?* or *You mean … ?***
   (**Clue: Use the Vocabulary words on page 46 to check.*)

2 **Now tell your partner what good things happened yesterday. Use these words:**

   baby   moved   future husband / wife   college

5.5 EXERCISE B GROUP C

Story C

Carla Jensen was a 19-year-old young woman from Denmark who worked as a servant. She traveled with her brother, uncle, and fiancé. They didn't have much money, so they traveled third class. They wanted to live in the U.S., but only Carla survived. Her family put her into the lifeboat because women went first. After the accident, she returned to Denmark and never left her country again.

PAIR WORK PRACTICE

5.5 EXERCISE B GROUP D

Story D

Charles Joughin, from the U.K., was 32 years old. He worked as a baker on the Titanic. He was one of the 212 crew members who survived. To escape, he jumped into the water and swam to a lifeboat. The water was very cold! The people on the lifeboat saw him and rescued him just in time. He became famous after the accident because of his amazing escape.

6.3 EXERCISE 4 STUDENT B

1   You want to buy something but you don't know the word for it in English. Choose one of the objects below and ask the salesperson for what you want.

2   You are now the salesperson. Your partner wants to buy something. Begin by asking if you can help.

This page is intentionally left blank

This page is intentionally left blank

This page is intentionally left blank

This page is intentionally left blank

This page is intentionally left blank

This page is intentionally left blank